CONTENTS

INDEX ON CENSORSHIP

VOLUME 45 NUMBER 3 – AUTUMN 2016

IN FOCUS

CULTURE

EDITOR
Rachael Jolley
DEPUTY EDITOR
Vicky Baker
SUB EDITORS
Alex Dudok de Wit, Jan Fox,
Sally Gimson
CONTRIBUTING EDITORS:
Irene Caselli (Argentina), Jan Fox (US),
Kaya Genç (Turkey), Natasha Joseph
(South Africa), Jemimah Steinfeld

EDITORIAL ASSISTANT
Josie Timms
DESIGN
Matthew Hasteley
COVER
Ben Jennings
THANKS TO:
Jodie Ginsberg, Sean Gallagher,
Ryan McChrystal

Magazine printed by Page Bros.,
Norwich, UK

Index on Censorship, 292 Vauxhall Bridge Road, London SW1V 1AE, United Kingdom
+44 (0) 20 7963 7262

Supported by
ARTS COUNCIL
ENGLAND

Anonymity matters

EDITORIAL

45(03): 03/05 | DOI: 10.1177/0306422016670327

by **Rachael Jolley**

Plans to ban fake names on social media could have wider implications for our right to anonymity, but it is a right worth fighting for

ANONYMITY IS OUT of fashion. There are plenty of critics who want it banned on social media. It's part of a harmful armoury of abuse, they argue.

Certainly, social media use seems to be doing its best to feed this argument. There are those anonymous trolls who sent vile verbal attacks to writers such as US author Lindy West. She was confronted by someone who actually set up a fake Twitter account under the name of her dead father.

Anonymity has been used in other ways by the unscrupulous. Earlier this year, a free messaging app called Kik was the method two young men used to get in touch with a 13-year-old girl, with whom they made friends online and then invited to meet. They were later charged with her murder. Participants who use Kik to chat do not have to register their real names or phone numbers, according to a report on the court case in the New York Times, which cited other current cases linked to Kik activity including using it to send child pornography.

So why do we need anonymity? Why does it matter? Why don't we just ban it or make it illegal if it can be used for all these harmful purposes? Anonymity is an integral part of our freedom of expression. For many people it is a valuable way of allowing them to speak. It protects from danger, and it allows those who wouldn't be able to speak or write to get the words out.

"If anonymity wasn't allowed any more, then I wouldn't use social media," a 14-year-old told me over the kitchen table a few weeks ago. He uses forums on the website Reddit to have debates about politics and religion, where he wants to express his view "without people underestimating my age".

Anonymity to this teenager is something that works for him; lets him operate in discussions where he wants to try out his arguments and gain experience in debates. Anonymity means no one judges who he is or his right to join in.

For others, using a fake or pen name adds a different layer of security. Writers for this magazine worry about their personal safety and sometimes ask for their names not to be carried on articles they write. In the current issue, an activist who works helping people find ways around China's internet restrictions is one of our authors who can't divulge his name because of the work he does.

Throughout history journalists have worked with sources who want to see important information exposed, but do not want their own identity to be made public. Look at the Watergate exposé or the Boston →

→ Globe investigation into child sex abuse by priests. Anonymous sources can provide essential evidence that helps keep an investigation on track.

That right, to keep sources private, has been the source of court actions against journalists through the years. And those who choose to work with journalists, often rely on that long-held practice.

Pen names, pseudonyms, fake identities

We must make sure that new systems aimed at tackling crime do not relinquish our right to anonymity

have all have been used for admirable and understandable purposes over the centuries: to protect someone's life; to blow a whistle on a crime; for a woman to get published at a period when only men did so, and on and on. Those who fought for democracy, the right to protest and other rights, often had to operate under the wire, out of the searching eyes of those who sought to stop them. Thomas Paine, who wrote the famous pamphlet Common Sense "Addressed to the Inhabitants of America", advocating the independence of the 13 states from Britain, first published his words in 1776 anonymously.

From the early days of Index on Censorship, when writing was being smuggled across borders and out of authoritarian countries, the need for anonymity was paramount.

Over the years it has been argued that anonymity is a vital component in the machinery of freedom of expression. While questions about using of false names on social media might seem very current, discussions have been rumbling along for several decades. In the USA, the American Civil Liberties Union argues that anonymity is a

First Amendment right, given in the Constitution. Back in 1996, in the US case of ACLU v Miller the ACLU won an injunction to prevent state enforcement of a statue that prohibited a person from sending email or posting to the internet under a false name.

Today, in India, the world's largest democracy, there are discussions about making anonymity unlawful. Our article by lawyer and writer Suhrith Parthasarathy considers why, if minister Maneka Gandhi does go ahead with plans to remove anonymity on Twitter, it could have ramifications for other forms of writing. As Anja Kovacs of the Internet Democracy Project told Index, "democracy virtually demands anonymity. It's crucial for both the protection of privacy rights and the right to freedom of expression".

We must make sure that new systems aimed at tackling crime do not relinquish our right to anonymity. Anonymity matters, let's remember it has a role to play. ⊗

Rachael Jolley
Editor, Index on Censorship

Follow the magazine @index_magazine

OPPOSITE: A caricature of Thomas Paine, whose pamphlets on US independence were published anonymously at first

** In the summer issue of the magazine we mistakenly referred to Mahatma Gandhi as a prime minister of India. While he is often referred to as "the father of the nation", and he led the Indian National Congress party, he was not a prime minister.

Credit: AKG

SPECIAL REPORT

LEFT: The Countess of Castiglione in a photo by Pierre-Louise Pierson, circa 1863/66

Credit: AKG

Under the wires

45(03): 8/11 | DOI: 10.1177/0306422016670328

Foreign correspondents often rely on "fixers" to help them report from war-torn countries. But, as **Caroline Lees** reveals, they can be targeted as spies if their names become known locally

RAWAND REGULARLY RISKS his life for strangers. The 25-year-old computer science student works as a fixer, a local journalist who supports foreign correspondents, in Erbil, Iraq. The city is only one hour's drive away from Mosul, which is occupied by IS. In June IS threatened to kill journalists "warring against Islam".

"Let's imagine IS comes to Erbil, the first people they will look for are the fixers," Rawand, who has worked with Vice News and Time magazine, said. "After every report the fixer remains in the country, while the reporter has a foreign passport and can leave," he added.

Fixers manage logistics for foreign correspondents, including translating and guiding, but they also research stories, develop contacts, arrange interviews and travel to front lines. Most are freelancers and are highly vulnerable to threats and reprisals, especially once their foreign colleagues leave. According to the Rory Peck Trust, an organisation which supports freelancers around the world, the number of local freelance journalists targeted for their work assisting international media is increasing.

"The majority of requests for our assistance comes from local freelancers who have been threatened, detained, imprisoned, attacked or forced into exile because of their work," Molly Clarke, head of communications at Rory Peck, said. "We regularly support those who have been targeted specifically because of their work with international media. And in these instances the consequences can be devastating and long-term – not just for them but their families too," Clarke added.

The Committee to Protect Journalists reports that 94 "media workers" have been killed since 2003: that was when the CPJ started to classify fixers separately in recognition of their growing importance to foreign news reporting. In June this year, Zabihullah Tamanna, an Afghan freelance journalist who was working as a translator for US's National Public Radio, was added to CPJ's list of those killed when the convoy he was travelling in was bombed in Afghanistan.

Many fixers start as inexperienced amateurs, desperate for paid work in economies damaged by conflict. They are rarely given training or long-term support by the international organisations they work for, and are often responsible for their own safety. Rawand has learnt to keep a low profile in Erbil. He seldom chooses to put his name on a report or article to which he has contributed. "Having my name attached to stories means I am not anonymous. There might be suspicion against me and I will be treated as a spy," he said.

Being accused of spying is an occupational hazard for many fixers working with foreign journalists. For those working on the front

OPPOSITE: Afghan journalists hold a picture of fixer Ajmal Naqshbandi, who was beheaded by the Taliban, at a protest in front of the Afghan parliament in Kabul April, 2007

line of the war between Ukraine and Russian-backed separatists it is a daily threat. In 2014, Anton Skiba, a local producer based in Donetsk, was abducted by separatists and accused of being a Ukrainian spy. He had spent the day working for CNN at the site where the Malaysian airlines flight MH17 crashed in separatist-held eastern Ukraine. Skiba, who has also worked for the BBC, was eventually freed, after a campaign by journalist colleagues. "It is really important to stay balanced while you have access to both sides of the conflict – otherwise there is a high chance of being oppressed by one of the sides," he said.

Skiba tries to protect himself by being careful about the people he works with and which stories he covers. "It is my country and I must continue to live here after journalists switch to another conflict. I do not

Only once I felt care from the international media. This May, one BBC colleague asked me if I needed support after my name was published on Myrotvorets

want to risk my life for a story which will be forgotten the next day. That's why I try to avoid journalists who are not professional or use fixers to get 'hot' stories," he said.

Another Donetsk fixer, Kateryna, obtained press accreditation from both the Ukrainian authorities and the opposing separatist Donetsk People's Republic to avoid accusations of favouring one side of the war over the other.

But this has not stopped the threats →

→ and harassment against her. She does not publicise that she works with international journalists but a Ukrainian website, Myrotvorets, recently revealed the names, email addresses and telephone numbers of around 5000 foreign and local journalists who have worked in the DPR and Luhansk – breakaway areas not controlled by the Ukrainian government. Kateryna, 28, was featured several times on the list, published in May 2016, because she has worked with the BBC, Al Jazeera and other media.

Kateryna has regularly been held and interrogated by Ukraine's security services because of her work. "After two years of work with foreign media you are in the security services' spotlight," she said. "And it is better not to underestimate their power. They are smart enough to play with your life."

She now feels exposed in Donetsk and would like to find other work. "Once a TV crew leaves, that's it," she said. "Only once I felt care from the international media. This May, one BBC colleague asked me if I needed support after my name was published on Myrotvorets. I refused any help because it was the least of what could happen to me."

It is my country and I must continue to live here after journalists switch to another conflict. I do not want to risk my life for a story which will be forgotten the next day

Few fixers are eligible for compensation if they are injured or killed while working. Nor are they given the de-facto international protection which is usually extended to foreign journalists working abroad. In Afghanistan alone, dozens of translators, drivers and local producers were killed between 2003

and 2011, some caught in fighting, others, including Ajmal Naqshbandi, a journalist, and Sayed Agha, a driver, were executed by the Taliban for working with foreigners.

Saira, a fixer in Kabul, Afghanistan for the last nine years, can only work if she hides not only her identity, but also herself. As a woman she is constantly threatened and abused. She is so fearful of retribution she would not give her real name for this article. The 26-year-old, who started working for foreign journalists to help fund her studies at Kabul university, said she only feels secure when her face is covered. "I have travelled to some risky places with foreign journalists. I had to fully cover my face with a burqa so I would feel safe," she said.

"It is always dangerous for a woman to work, even in Kabul, they get bad comments from society and no respect. Many people blame you and even call you infidel as you work with a non-Muslim," Saira said.

Fixers in conflict zones considered too dangerous for foreign reporters are increasingly being hired to write and file stories directly to international news desks. "There is a greater reliance on local freelancers for stories, news and images in countries and areas where it is difficult – or too dangerous – for [international reporters] to gain access," said Clarke. "We don't have any specific facts or figures, our evidence is mostly anecdotal from what we've heard and observed through our work."

Almigdad Mojalli was a fixer who became a reporter when war in Yemen forced many foreigners to leave the country. Mojalli, 34, spoke good English, knew the right people, was respected and in demand.

Mojalli preferred to work anonymously. "He liked being a fixer because it allowed him to tell stories he couldn't safely tell in Yemen," said Laura Battaglia, an Italian journalist who worked with him and became his friend. "With his agreement we kept his name off difficult articles, to protect him."

But when Mojalli started reporting alone

he encountered problems with the Houthi militia, a rebel group which controlled Sana'a, Yemen's capital. Almost his very first story, filed to newsdesks in Europe and the US under his own name, angered the establishment. He was immediately arrested and threatened by government agents. In January this year he was killed in an airstrike while on assignment for Voice of America. He was travelling in a dangerous area in an unmarked car with no indication that he was a journalist.

Mojalli's death also raised questions of responsibility. He was a freelancer, but working in the field for international news organisations. Mike Garrod, co-founder of World Fixer, an online network that links local journalists and freelancers with international reporters, believes some media groups are starting to take their role in the safety of the freelancers they employ more seriously.

Garrod hopes to set up an online training programme for local journalists and fixers. The course will include risk assessment, security and journalistic standards and ethics. "Fixers are largely untrained and vulnerable in hostile environments. As their use as more than just translators and logistics becomes more prevalent there is a real need for them to understand, and be able to prove they understand certain concepts," Garrod said. The BBC, CNN and Reuters were asked about their fixers' policies for this article. None of them choose to comment.

However, the behaviour of some individual journalists who employ fixers in the field is harder to regulate, according to Garrod. He related the story of a young student, hired by a foreign reporter to go to Iraq's front line when he was 17. "There is so much the industry can do to encourage journalists to act more responsibly in regards to this, but I worry the will is not there to scrutinise how a story is gathered," he said.

Zia Ur Rehman, 35, worked with foreign correspondents in Karachi, Pakistan, between 2011 and 2015. He said that while local journalists in the city understand the dangers facing journalists there, some foreign reporters ignore their advice. "Some cameramen and photographers are bad-mannered and rude and treat the fixer as their servants. As they do not know the complexity and sensitivity of situation, they make films or take photos without consulting the fixer and it has caused big problems for the team,

Saira, a fixer in Kabul, Afghanistan for the last nine years, can only work if she hides not only her identity, but also herself

especially for the fixer," Rehman said.

There have been cases where fixers have been abducted, beaten and even tortured by Pakistan's security services because of their work with foreign journalists. Rehman said he rarely works as a fixer anymore, if he does it will only be for a reporter he knows.

More training and support from international organisations employing fixers is crucial to their safety, but it is unlikely to make a difference in areas still controlled by IS, which is determined to silence journalists, especially those working with foreign outlets. In June this year the CPJ reported that IS had executed five freelance journalists in Syria. One was tied to his laptop, another to his camera, both packed with explosives and then detonated. They had been accused of working with foreign news and human rights organisations. IS released videos of their killings as a warning to others. ⊗

Caroline Lees is a former south Asia correspondent for the UK's Sunday Times. She is currently research officer at the Reuters Institute for the Study of Journalism at the University of Oxford

*Some names in this article have been changed for security reasons

Art attack

45(03): 12/16 | DOI: 10.1177/0306422016670329

The growing popularity of Chinese art has been both a blessing and a curse. As major art exhibitions open across the world, **Jemimah Steinfeld** finds out why China's artists are under pressure

CHINESE ART IS booming. Art villages have mushroomed across the country, serving an increasing local demand. But this interest in Chinese art isn't confined to China itself, it is a global phenomenon. In 2011, Pablo Picasso and Andy Warhol lost their titles as the highest-selling artists in the world to Chinese artists Qi Baishi and Zhang Daqian.

For outspoken artists, the higher profile of Chinese art can work in their favour. The international outcry at the artist Ai Weiwei's arrest is testament to this. His reputation brought world attention to his imprisonment, and he was freed.

Equally though, increased popularity can mean restrictions on artists. While art has never been completely removed from the political in China, its niche status meant that it was lower down on the list of industries about which the censors cared. TV, radio and cinema, all media with mass appeal, were more closely scrutinised. Now as galleries across the country attract significant footfall and the position of the artists within Chinese society is elevated, the authorities are paying closer attention to what artists are doing.

For an exhibition to take place in China today, curators must get approval from the government. A curator at one of the biggest galleries in Beijing, who requested anonymity, explained to Index how galleries must submit censorship lists, titles and descriptions of all the works they proposes to exhibit in public.

"[President] Xi is very authoritarian. Until recently the art market was not that affected by this because it was very small with little influence. That is starting to change. The government is overseeing public museums more carefully today than they did in the past as a result of more popularity," the curator said.

How the government is responding to artists who seek to provoke is less clear. Last year Ai Weiwei was suddenly given his passport back and able to travel. It was a surprising shift after his imprisonment and attempts

by the Chinese authorities to disrupt his work and intimidate those who promoted him after he was freed.

Other artists have found themselves under relentless attack. Recent years have seen arrests, alongside calls on artists to promote socialism in their work – a sentiment that led to China's censors, in the form of the State Administration of Press, Publication,

As the position of artists is elevated the authorities are paying closer attention to what artists are doing

Radio, Film and TV suggesting artists should be sent to live in rural areas so they could "form a correct view of art". It all sounded reminiscent of the cultural revolution.

Some have suggested the return of Ai's passport was a subtle way of asking the provocative artist to leave China altogether.

Joyce Yu-Jean Lee, an artist who has worked in Beijing, thinks differently. "What is happening right now is intentionally erratic," she told Index. "With Xi it's very aggressive and the patterns are less obvious, so everyone is on their guard constantly," she added to explain why sometimes the authorities are very harsh and other times they appear more lenient.

Speaking to people across China's art community, from artists through to curators, this erratic pattern is palpable. Zhang Dali, one of the most high profile artists from modern China, describes censorship as becoming "less and less" today. But a spokesperson for the well-known LWH Gallery in Shanghai, which has a reputation for collaborating with Tibetan artists, said working with Tibetans had become tougher of late.

Coupled with a changing political climate is a changing economy and this is also playing a role in censorship. →

ILLUSTRATION: Red Pepper

Money being invested in art has led to the rise of self-censorship as artists "sell out" to commercial interests. The artist Zhang highlights an important shift since his early career in the late 1980s and early 1990s. "At the time we were very interested in philosophy and in politics. There was no consumerism. Now young people are more interested in how to change their own life. They are not so interested in common or public problems. Life is very expensive."

Contemporary Chinese art made its debut in a very different context when the country was a lot less wealthy and money-orientated. In many ways it was born out of a struggle

The artists' efforts paid off. The government allowed them to exhibit their work in some of the most important art institutions in China. The 1980s were seen as an important period of freedom, experimentation and growth for Chinese art.

That said, openness was only tolerated up to a point. In February 1989, for example, a Beijing show China/Avant-Garde, which displayed highlights of China's art movement of the 1980s, was closed down on the same day it opened.

Shortly after came the violent crushing of the student-led demonstrations on Tiananmen Square. In the aftermath several

But others, fearful for their lives, muted their opinions or fled the country altogether

for free speech. Most people attribute its arrival to 1979. On 27 September of that year, three years after the death of Mao Zedong and the end of the cultural revolution, a group of young artists displayed their work outside the National Art Gallery in Beijing. These works were bold, influenced largely by Western modernism, an artistic style that had been forbidden during the Mao years when artwork was subservient to political dogma.

Within two days, the week-long exhibition was shut down. The artists and their supporters responded by holding a demonstration. One of the leading artists, Wang Keping, a sculptor, brandished a placard with five characters on it: Want art freedom.

It was a defining moment – the first time in China that artists had challenged Communist Party censorship, rather than kowtowing to it. The group of artists were dubbed the "Stars Group", as they were thought to be like stars in the night sky, struggling to be seen and heard.

BEYOND BORDERS

Censorship of Chinese art is no longer confined to works on show in China

Artist Joyce Yu-Jean Lee's exhibition was never going to be embraced by the Chinese government. The idea was to create a pop-up internet café in Chinatown, New York. It would look like a regular cafe, except all the computers' internet connections would run through a Chinese server. After browsing online for some time punters would likely come across the commonplace page on the Chinese internet – 404 error.

Lee, who had worked with artists in China in the past, was interested in how censorship affected creative output for ordinary people and for artists. She wanted to raise awareness of this and hence her art project FIREWALL Internet Café was born.

It was timed to open during Chinese New Year 2016 and to close on the first anniversary of the arrest of five prominent Chinese feminists, in early March. One week ahead of its official opening, a panel discussion was scheduled to act as a soft opening. The discussion, Networked Feminism in China, avant-garde artists adopted cynical realism in their work, seen to exemplify the disillusionment with Chinese society. But others, fearful for their lives, muted their opinions or fled the country altogether. This chilling effect, combined with an increasingly affluent population, changed the game.

And yet today it is not just Ai Weiwei who refuses to play by the rules. Ren Hang is another example. Ren is one of China's most provocative artists and co-curated a show with Ai in 2013. Like Ai, he is no stranger to the authorities. They have threatened to arrest him and, as he told Index, plenty of his work has never been shown publically. His website is constantly banned. Still, he continues his work and says that he would never self-censor.

Unlike Ai, Ren's work is not political. His signature photographs blend nature with nudity. This work falls under another category banned in China: pornography. Since the ascent of the Chinese Communist Party in 1949, pornography or obscene content has been forbidden under Chinese law. In fact, the most common censorship of art is within the moral sphere. For most of Mao's era, displays of nudity were forbidden. Even today, nudity and sexuality are sensitive topics. →

included several high-profile Chinese figures, including Lu Pin, a feminist who lives in the USA. Another participant was a Chinese lawyer still based in China.

As sensitive as these topics might be in China, Lee never thought she would have a problem discussing them in New York. But the night before the panel discussion, the lawyer was contacted by her boss back in China. Officials had heard about the talk and wanted her name to be removed from it.

"She was basically banned from being part of my project," Lee told Index.

"Her participation was auxiliary and the project was in New York, so I was very surprised," she added.

Nevertheless, Lee took her name out of the project, which involved deleting all social media.

"It was very strange doing a project on censorship and to be censoring – it was the antithesis of what our aims were. But we take security very seriously," she said.

All of those involved assumed this was the end. It was not. The threats started to escalate and it became clear that there would be serious ramifications. Lee did not want to divulge more information out of fear it could compromise the participant further.

The event took place with different speakers. As for the cafe, it still opened, just with everyone on guard.

"I was told there might be plain clothes government officials in the audience. We were very cautious after that, not speaking as openly as we would have liked," said Lee, who even eschewed an invitation to speak on Voice of America, an opportunity she would have ordinarily leapt at.

A few months on, Lee is still wondering why her exhibition and its events were in the firing line. She has a few theories – that the government was watching and scrutinising feminists more in the lead-up to the anniversary; that lawyers are currently under attack in China and it was part of a tactic to keep them at bay; or that it was to do with her connections with freedom of expression activists.

"So perhaps a partnership with them was problematic," she said.

There are no certainties, except that the Chinese government is paying far more attention to its reputation abroad than ever before, and exercising a lot more muscle to control it.

JS

ABOVE: Sculptor
Wang Keping and Ai
Weiwei in Paris in
January 2016

The curator also reveals that there are secret rooms in many of the top galleries, used when art is considered too political

→ However, there are subtle ways to circumvent censorship.

"You can present a different version of the exhibition to the one that will be on display. That's a common practise," explained the anonymous curator, who believes that a lot of the censors are not educated enough in art to understand the nuances and messages of the work. The curator also reveals that there are secret rooms in many of the top galleries, used when art is considered too political.

"If we sense something is very political, we put it in a private space," the curator told Index, citing examples of several major artists whose work has been shown privately. It's a concession to be sure, but at least it is something.

All of this goes a long way in explaining why, despite today's opaque censorship and the pressures of commercialism, experimental and irreverent Chinese art exists, as do bold, brave artists. Of course not all good art needs to be political or sexual. For those artists who choose that path though, there are ways to exhibit both at home and abroad. ⊗

Jemimah Steinfeld is a contributing editor to Index. She previously reported for CNN and Time Out from Beijing

JOURNALISTS REPORTED **42** ATTACKS TO PROPERTY IN Q2 2016.

Mapping Media Freedom collated and verified a total of 341 reports of violations of press freedom across Europe and neighbouring countries between April and June 2016 (Q2). The platform was founded by Index on Censorship in May 2014. You can read the latest report at Mappingmediafreedom.org

CO-FUNDED BY THE

Naming names

45(03): 18/22 I DOI: 10.1177/0306422016670331

India has created a new "cyber cell" for tackling trolls that attack women online. But, **Suhrith Parthasarathy** asks, if people are no longer allowed to use pseudonyms, will an important freedom disappear?

"I want to remove anonymity on Twitter, as well," Gandhi said last December, in an interview with a news channel, where she spoke about the prospect of online policing. "You should be responsible for what you say and the consequences that follow." Although the presently established cell would not specifically target anonymous users, the

Law enforcement in all countries tends to make citizens believe that anonymity is somehow harmful. But democracy virtually demands anonymity

fear is that any move which ultimately seeks to regulate the internet would harm the right to remain anonymous of both dissenters and members of marginalised communities. Maintaining a veil of anonymity allows people to speak freely, unhindered by a fear of a backlash from either the state or from the society at large.

"I really appreciate that Maneka Gandhi has taken up this issue. There is a real problem with online abuse, but we have to be careful how we tackle this," Anja Kovacs, the director of the Delhi-based think-tank Internet Democracy Project told Index. "Law enforcement in all countries tends to make citizens believe that anonymity is somehow harmful. But democracy virtually demands anonymity. It's crucial for both the protection of privacy rights and the right to freedom of expression. So any initiative that seeks to police the internet mustn't make anonymity impossible."

The importance of protecting anonymous speech in a democracy was perhaps best stated by the US Supreme Court in a 1995 ruling, McIntyre v. Ohio Elections Commission.

"Anonymity is a shield from the tyranny of the majority," Justice John Paul →

THE RIGHT TO anonymity is under threat in India. Being anonymous online is said by politicians to be harmful, giving trolls free rein to attack women without being identified. But some see anonymity as an essential democratic right and fear what will happen if it disappears.

In July, India's women and child development minister, Maneka Gandhi, announced the creation of a new "cyber cell", a government committee that will monitor instances of women being abused by online trolls.

MAIN: Protesters from the Anonymous India group of hackers wear Guy Fawkes masks in Mumbai in 2012

→ Stevens wrote for the majority. "[...] It thus exemplifies the purpose behind the Bill of Rights and of the First Amendment in particular: to protect unpopular individuals from retaliation [...] at the hand of an intolerant society."

In some ways article 19(1)(a) of India's Constitution mirrors the US Constitution's First Amendment. It guarantees its citizens a right to free speech and expression. But the following clause, article 19(2), permits the state to make "reasonable restrictions" on the right in the interests, among other things, of morality, sovereignty and integrity of the state, public order, friendly relations with foreign states, and so forth. It is this limiting clause, which is often used to justify restraints on expression. And Kovacs is not the only one who thinks anonymity is a

Women write through pseudonyms, out of fear induced by their families and because of societal norms

vital right that could be under threat. Frank La Rue, then UN special rapporteur on the promotion and protection of the right to freedom of opinion and expression, said, in 2011, anonymity was critical to the protection of privacy and free speech rights.

In India, legitimate speech has often been curtailed by the government on grounds that, at best, can be described as inconveniencing the state, by invoking the limiting clause in article 19(2). Is anonymity next on this list?

There is a worry that, under the guise of protecting women and other marginalised sections from abusive trolling, these limitations would no longer allow anonymity. Rega Jha, the editor of BuzzFeed India, who has been subjected to vast amounts of abuse on social media in the past, expressed particular scepticism of systems aimed at combatting trolling.

"India doesn't have a good track record of appropriately using well-intentioned laws intended to protect its citizens online," she said. "Even laws intended to protect women have ended up manifesting as boundaries on freedom of expression ... If the state is empowered to bring people out of anonymity for committing crimes online, anonymity's function in safeguarding freedom of expression is rendered basically useless."

In India, as Kovacs pointed out, it isn't merely the fear of the state that makes the protection of anonymity important. There are women and members from others marginalised groups who blog and tweet anonymously. They write through pseudonyms, out of fear induced by their families, and because of the societal norms. In 2013, the IDP think-tank spoke to a number of women who blog and tweet anonymously with a view to avoiding confrontations with family and peers. "Tripti, a young blogger talks about her experiences on Facebook – where she is not anonymous – as 'stressful', given the 'pressure of judgement' and that 'people don't take kindly to frank opinions.'" The report observes: "In this way, her blog, which she runs under a pseudonym, 'frees her' from these pressures. Through these examples, it is possible to see that women may choose to be anonymous online as a direct consequence of the abuse or harassment."

One anonymous blogger, who uses the pseudonym @GabbbarSingh on Twitter told Index it wasn't originally a conscious choice of his to remain anonymous. "It was like any other parody handle primarily for comic relief," he said. "When the followership grew, there was this itch to come out and revel in this new found online fame ... But at the same time I realised the powers of anonymity. And chose to remain so, as it gave me a 'soft immunity' from my employers, partners and family."

Particularly when making points of political interest, @GabbbarSingh said he often receives criticism for remaining →

Credit: Eva Bee

evabee

→ anonymous. "A common refrain is: can you say that without hiding behind the cloak of anonymity?," he said. "But that's often when the debater runs out of arguments." While he recognises that anonymity can have harmful consequences, when it's used as a means to troll and abuse other users online, @GabbbarSingh believes that state control of the internet can be a double-edged sword.

This is because, in India, systems aimed at tackling crime on the internet often tend to strike at anonymity. Kovacs cited the example of the draft encryption policy released by the Indian government's department of electronics and information technology in September last year. "They have since withdrawn these draft rules after a lot of protest from activists," said Kovacs. "But it's clear they wanted encryption to be weak. For ex-

A common refrain is: can you say that without hiding behind the cloak of anonymity?

ample, the policy to force people to store all encrypted information for 90 days, if implemented as law, would substantially weaken anonymity and internet user security."

There is in India today no law, as instructed by the UN special rapporteur on freedom of expression, which specifically recognises that individuals are free to protect the privacy of their digital communications by using encryption and anonymity tools. This gives rise to fears that measures such as Maneka Gandhi's, which are aimed at a larger policing of the internet, could damage the rights of people who want to maintain their anonymity. Although there might be circumstances in which the state can lawfully intervene to force someone to come out of a cloak of anonymity, there is a belief that such powers could be exploited to protect the private interests of government. Drawing

a proper balance, therefore, between protecting anonymity and fighting abusive trolls, becomes a tricky exercise.

"The state could demand compromised anonymity because it perceives a 'crime' in someone tweeting threats, sure, but also if it chooses to perceive a 'crime' in someone criticising a ruling party, expressing homosexuality, political dissent, or any of an array of inconvenient national truths," Jha told Index. "It feels like if this power exists, anonymity wouldn't serve its noblest purpose in a democracy anymore – allowing citizens to express the important truths that are dangerous to voice with a name and face attached."

Lawyer and free speech expert Gautam Bhatia provides an answer to this apparent impasse. According to him, the only principled way to tackle hate speech on the internet, while preserving a larger right to anonymity, would be to grant the judiciary powers to look beyond the veil of anonymity when a person abuses his or her anonymity to engage in illegal speech. He suggests a procedure similar to that adopted by the court authorised by the US Foreign Intelligence Surveillance Act, which decides on a case-by-case basis whether to award a warrant for executive surveillance. "You can have a dedicated lawyer to oppose demands for de-anonymising, like what was proposed for the American FISA court," Bhatia told me. "The default should be that you lose the protection of anonymity when you engage in unlawful speech; [but] it should not be the other way round, that you lose the protection of anonymity in order to prevent you from potentially engaging in unlawful speech." ⊗

Suhrith Parthasarathy is based in Chennai, India, and is a regular contributor to Index. He is a lawyer and writer. He tweets @suhrith

Secrets and spies

45(03): 23/25 | DOI: 10.1177/0306422016670332

Former CIA officer **Valerie Plame Wilson** argues that secrecy and
anonymity are sometimes vitally important

ANONYMITY: IT CAPTURES the very essence of life and work in the CIA. The agency could not function without it. As a former covert CIA operations officer, I know how anonymity is used – and misused – as well as the valid reasons for it within the national security context.

Secrecy, discretion and, above all, the protection of assets is tightly woven into the agency's DNA. The very notion of anonymity and its cousin secrecy chaffs at some who see their use as wholly incompatible within a democracy. Our world is still coming to terms with the consequences of Wikileaks and Snowden disclosures, the near weekly cyber hacks of private information from corporations and government alike, the

significant spike in worldwide terrorist activity and the security services' inability to stop them. The role of anonymity in the collection of intelligence and the attendant risk to democratic values need balancing.

The CIA is often used as a convenient scapegoat for the abuse of secrecy in the 21st century. Its failures and successes in some ways serve as a weathervane to judge how societies at large view the increasing application of secrets across all aspects of our lives. It is therefore instructive to begin with an overview of the CIA's use and justifications of secrecy.

To accomplish its mission of providing accurate and informed intelligence to policymakers, CIA officers working in the field →

ABOVE: Former CIA operative Valerie Plame Wilson testifies, in March 2007, at the House Oversight and Government Reform Committee's hearing on the leaking of her identity

→ employ a variety of covers of varying depth to conduct their operations securely. That is, they ostensibly work for companies or other entities in order to live and travel internationally. While gathering intelligence and recruiting spies they play "the grey man" (or woman), outwardly boring, able to blend into a crowd while simultaneously working it. Secrecy, inherent to covert action, provides the US government "plausible deniability", which is useful in keeping diplomatic channels open and intact when secrets are being exchanged.

The agency has a long-standing policy prohibiting the use of journalists, the clergy or NGOs for cover purposes. These entities have made it abundantly clear over the decades that any CIA affiliation – real or perceived – would irrevocably harm and undermine their work and reputations internationally. Nonetheless, in 1997 the US Congress inserted language into a bill allowing the president or the director of central intelligence to waive this policy when deemed essential. There have been some occasions when the CIA has ventured into these arenas for cover purposes, but it generally didn't end well. Legitimate interests were compromised.

Working under cover, my anonymity meant everything to me. Unlike those in military uniform or diplomats who are well known to local intelligence services, I moved around cities with relative ease. Taking

The life of a spy: a timeline

By JOSIE TIMMS

1985: Valerie Plame Wilson joins the CIA, and spends the next two decades working on national security and the prevention of the spread of weapons of mass destruction.

JULY 2003: Washington Post writer Robert Novak reveals that Plame Wilson is a CIA operative in an article on how her husband, Joseph C Wilson, visited Niger in 2002 to investigate the alleged sale of uranium to Iraq. Wilson had deemed the sale unlikely, which conflicted with President George W Bush's decision to go to war on the grounds that Iraq's President Saddam Hussein had nuclear weapons. Wilson had also written in The New York Times, earlier in July, that he believed intelligence had been "twisted".

DECEMBER 2003: An inquiry begins to investigate whether the exposure of Plame Wilson's identity was a violation of federal law and whether White House officials were involved in the leak. The inquiry includes the questioning of President Bush, Vice President Dick Cheney, adviser Karl Rove and vice-presidential aide I. Lewis "Scooter" Libby.

JULY 2006: Plame Wilson and her husband file a lawsuit against Cheney, Rove and Libby, accusing the officials of violating their constitutional rights.

MARCH 2007: Libby was found guilty of lying about his role in leaking Plame Wilson's identity, making him the highest-ranking White House official to be be convicted of a felony in nearly 20 years. The jury found him guilty of four of five counts of obstruction, perjury and lying to the FBI.

JUNE 2007: Libby receives a 30-month prison sentence and a US$250,000 fine.

JULY 2007: President Bush commutes Libby's sentence, and he is instead given two years' probation and the US$250,000 fine.

certain precautions, I met with assets, or potential ones, without attracting undue, unwanted attention. For the most part, it looked like a typical date to the casual observer.

Even more importantly, the foreigners whom CIA officers seek to recruit to do the actual spying and obtain secrets – the assets – must likewise be protected with anonymity by the use of code names or cryptonyms. Only essential CIA officials with a genuine "need to know" are able to see the true names of these assets. The reason for this is obvious; if assets were known to be co-operating with US intelligence, it could be fatal for themselves and their families. An early example of the value of anonymity is Eduard Schulte, a prominent German industrialist who travelled frequently to Switzerland during World War ll and was the first to report to the CIA about the Nazi's "Final Solution" using concentration camps. Had Schulte's identity been known, he would have been killed.

The motivations for spying are as varied and vast as there are individuals themselves. From financial concerns, to ideological affiliations, egotistical yearnings, and every combination between, the CIA officer's first job is to determine the right combination of these to recruit a spy and run him in a secure operation. While it is abundantly true that the CIA is not the Boy Scouts and some of its assets are deeply flawed human beings in all the ways that humans can be, my experience has been that CIA officers hold as dogma the absolute need to protect their sources and methods. If one fails at that, the consequences are profound.

The most critical question facing Western democracies today is the appropriate balance of security versus privacy. There has always been a historic dynamic tension between the two poles, but since 9/11 and the Iraq war the stark contrast between the two and defenders of each has never been greater. Is meaningful accountability of secret government programmes even possible without compromising legitimate national

security needs? It is, but the judiciary, in an automatic reflex, sides with the government and its claimed national security needs. It is time to embolden and support independence and skepticism in the judiciary to truly weigh the issues at hand within the context of the Fourth Amendment.

On a personal note, I took my anonymity for granted until it was abruptly ripped away by senior Bush White House officials in 2003 in the service of a nakedly partisan agenda. I found Andy Warhol's prediction that in the future, "everyone will be world famous for 15 minutes" to be mortifying. Professional satisfaction in my CIA job came from my colleagues' acknowledgement. Finding myself to be a public figure in the wake of the political scandal was deeply disorienting. And, of course, after my CIA affiliation was betrayed, continuing my covert operations was impossible. In a world of nation-states, of conflicts and deeply different goals, obtaining intelligence is a necessary reality. Anonymity is an essential ingredient in that effort and I was proud to be part of it. ⊗

Valerie Plame Wilson is a former CIA operative. She is married to the former US ambassador Joseph Wilson. Her identity became public in the "CIA leak scandal" during the George W Bush administration, after her husband criticised the government. Her book Fair Game was also turned into a film starring Sean Penn

ABOVE: A 2007 protest against President Bush commuting the prison sentence of I. Lewis "Scooter" Libby

Undercover artist

45(03): 26/29 | DOI:10.1177/0306422016670333

Los Angeles graffiti artist **Skid Robot** works to change the lives of homeless people in the city. **Jan Fox** speaks to him about his street art and why he does not want anyone to know his identity

WHAT DO BANKSY, Charlotte Brontë, Daft Punk and JK Rowling have in common? They've all chosen anonymity at some point in their artistic careers.

Writing as Currer Bell, Brontë hoped she would be taken more seriously if readers didn't know she was a woman. JK Rowling attempted to remain incognito as a crime novelist by publishing under the name of Robert Galbraith. Historically, fear of persecution has also led to artists and writers choosing to wear a mask.

So in a data-driven, Instagram-rich world, how hard is it to preserve anonymity as an artist and how far does that anonymity force us to look more closely at the message in the art, rather than at the artists themselves?

On any given night in Los Angeles, a young man with a spray can is attempting to highlight the problem of homelessness in the city. Skid Robot paints tiki huts and palm trees, living rooms, bedrooms, thrones and leafy forests behind living subjects in an attempt to give humanity to the

ABOVE: Birdman, one of Skid Robot's most celebrated subjects, had lived under a freeway for more than 20 years

CREDIT: Skid Robot

estimated 8,000 dejected and forgotten men and women who live on the city streets, concentrated in a 54 block area of downtown known as Skid Row. They are part of the county's record 47,000 homeless.

Skid Robot, whose name is a mash-up of the area he's trying to draw attention to and the toy company Kid Robot, has been working on the streets for two-and-a-half years in what he calls a Living Art Project.

Already a graffiti artist, he'd been looking for more purpose to his work. Out on a date night with his girlfriend, he found it when sitting at a red traffic light in downtown LA's Skid Row area.

"The conversation we were having was about the lack of quality in street art in LA – that it was more like marketing, done to post on social media – rather than artistic. I felt it devalued art. So I was yearning for a new way to express myself," said Robot.

"My girlfriend drew my notice to a homeless person sleeping on the floor and said I should draw a dream bubble over her head so I grabbed my spray can and jumped out and drew a bubble with a bag of money inside it and that was the seed of the project."

The work quickly progressed to intricate paintings with a lot more gravitas, often with added furniture to create full installations, with his subjects posing in new roles as homeowners sitting on sofas, reclining on beds, or in tents surrounded by trees in a forest. Robot transported those living on the streets, albeit fleetingly, away from the grimy reality of a gloomy underpass or street corner.

"I saw a man in a wheelchair one day. We're all kings and queens, so I painted him on a throne in a very active part of Skid Row. It made him feel good as people passed by and noticed him. It gave him a sense of his worth," said Robot. "The artwork takes them to a different reality. We make friends and find positivity through art."

"One of the elements is obviously that graffiti is illegal but also it's because what

Skid Robot is doing is more important than what I'm doing," he said.

"We live in a vain and shallow society and maybe if some people find out I'm a particular race, say, and they have a bigotry of any kind, that may dilute the message and the art is the message. It's not about who I am or what I look like."

Skid Robot's name is a mash-up of Skid Row, the area he's trying to draw attention to, and the toy company Kid Robot

Some of Robot's off-the-beaten-track works are still visible around the LA streets, but most get swiftly removed by the city. The ephemeral nature of such anonymous art is not a problem for him though. "In a sense, it's only living art while the subject is still with the artwork – once they get up and →

LEFT: Skid Robot's installation Under a Bridge Downtown. J.W., pictured in the photograph, is also an artist

I can't be sure of everyone so there's always that risk, but if people do find out who I am, it won't change what I'm doing. There's a kind of cops-and-robbers excitement

→ move away, it changes anyway," he said.

The art, though ephemeral, can have a lasting effect. One of Robot's most celebrated subjects was Birdman, who'd lived under the freeway for more than 20 years.

"The living room installation I made him, gave him the gift of feeling he had a home – he hadn't shaved or cut his hair in 15 or 20 years. Within a week he had cut his hair. He found a non-profit that helped him into an apartment. It all came about through art and the friendship that we created together," said Robot.

The biggest threat to Robot's anonymity? "Arrest, clearly, because graffiti is illegal."

So far, he's been lucky, though he's had a few close calls. He was painting down by the LA river one night and some cops showed up. Robot backed away, tossed his paint and played drunk but was caught literally red-handed – with paint on them. He thought the game was up as he was loaded into the back of the police car, then realised the cops were looking at the work – a tiki hut and palm trees – and laughing. It wasn't a gang tag, just a pretty picture. They let him go.

But if his luck runs out, he's prepared for it. "I'm not afraid of arrest if it's worth it to bring even more attention to the project," said Robot.

So why does no one give him or other anonymous artists away?

"I think no one wants to go down in history as 'the rat', to be labelled as that," he laughed. "I'm careful – I can't be sure of everyone so there's always that risk, but if people do find out who I am, it won't change what I'm doing. There's a kind of cops-and-robbers excitement around what I'm doing and graffiti is illegal, but some of it enhances our environment so there are people who enjoy that and wouldn't want to give me away. We are creating an impact. If we are telling stories this way we can start to change things and I think a lot of people value that," he said.

"Thousands of commuters drove through

that underpass every day and saw Birdman and the fake room and they started to look for it and it created a memory. Eventually we put a tiny house there and I bought fake grass and a lawn chair. Then the city took the tiny house and so I tagged [Los Angeles mayor] Eric Garcetti's name with the message: 'You can take a man's home but not his spirit'.

"The mayor responded on my Instagram! To know he acknowledged it and felt he had to respond revved it up. We got his attention.

"I started this project from the heart and I was passionate about it artistically. This [Skid Row] was such a chaotic place that I was compelled to do something about those who are ignored and marginalised," he said.

"It started with people and dream bubbles and continues to evolve. My aim is to provide shipping container homes painted by artists, a Bauhaus-type mentality combining art, design and technology. It's not a permanent solution but will surely do in a crisis like this.

"A big part of the anonymity angle is that I'm trying to say to people to treat other people as you want to be treated, save humanity. It isn't just homelessness that's the issue. We might lose a lot of our freedom because of the way political leaders are acting. Our apathy to this is the same as the apathy that might goose-step us into war again one day in the not too distant future," said Robot.

Despite what he sees as lack of real action by the city of LA to tackle the homeless issue overall, he's optimistic. "A hundred per cent. We can have a flourishing reality through the Living Art project. There are plenty of angles to work and plenty of people with heart including artists, musicians, architects. It's like a ship or a rocket. I hope people will jump on and we'll create that new frontier through the human spirit," he said.

"The mask of anonymity is important because it's the living art that takes precedence, not me, but if I have to come out from behind the mask at some point because

it would further the solution, that's what would have to happen. It isn't like I'm a Banksy who thinks: 'I'm anonymous because I'm cool'. It's because I am the people and I have to connect with the people to get the message out and create change." ⊗

Find out more about Skid Robot's Living Art Project at skid-robot.com

Jan Fox *is a writer and actor based in Los Angeles, and is a contributing editor to Index on Censorship magazine*

ABOVE AND OPPOSITE: A selection of Skid Robot's works from his Living Art Project, taken on the streets of Los Angeles

A meeting at Trolls Anonymous

45(03): 30/31 I DOI: 10.1177/0306422016670334

What happens when aggressive, nameless social media users meet face to face? **John Crace** imagines a confessional get-together between trolls as they take a break from exchanging insults and death threats

"HI," HE SAID. "My name's Colin and I'm a troll."

"Hello Colin," everyone replied.

"Welcome to the Wednesday night meeting of Trolls Anonymous. In Trolls Anonymous we believe that by sharing our hope and experience we can help each other to lead a troll-free life. Is there anyone who would like to start the meeting?"

"Yes, please. My name's Ian and I'm a troll."

"Hi Ian."

"This is very difficult for me to share, but I'm afraid I've had a relapse since last week. I still don't really know what went wrong. One moment I was just sitting at home reading an article about some woman Labour MP who was getting death threats and I was even beginning to feel some sympathy for her. Then it was like a switch clicked in my brain and the next thing I knew I had logged in to my Twitter account @KeepBritain_English and had sent this woman a tweet saying, 'Stop the War or die, you bitch'. Before I knew it, several hours had passed and I was busy insulting all Muslims and had received a death threat myself from @Israel4Allah."

"Thank you for sharing that, Ian. Can anyone identify with Ian?"

"My name's Barry and I'm a troll."

"Hi Barry."

"I wasn't actually going to say anything tonight, but Ian's sharing has made me want to speak. Over the six months I've been coming to TA, Ian and I have become really good friends and every Saturday night we go off down to the pub together but it's only now that I've come to realise he's @KeepBritain_English. I feel really guilty about this because I am @Israel4Allah and every time he slips out to the toilet, his is one of the Twitter accounts I love to troll. As soon as he leaves the bar, I just can't help myself. I get out my phone and tweet the most obscene things that come to mind followed by #gobacktowhereyoucamefromyouNazifuck #genderfluidrefugee. When Ian comes back from the lav I

pretend I've just been checking the football scores on my phone and then we go back to talking about the government's mishandling of the junior doctor's strike. So I'd like to take this opportunity to say sorry."

"That's a very brave thing of you to share, Barry," said Colin. "Maybe it would be a good idea if you could both help one another to delete your Twitter accounts. Now I see we have a newcomer in the room. Is there anything you would like to say?

"I'm @TheRealDonaldTrump."

"I'm sorry @TheRealDonaldTrump, but we don't use Twitter handles in the room. At Trolls Anonymous we only believe in certain levels of anonymity. So perhaps you could introduce yourself using your real first name."

In Trolls Anonymous, we believe that by sharing our hope and experience we can help each other to lead a troll-free life

"Hi, I'm Donald."

"And do you identify yourself as a troll?"

"Hell no. I identify myself as the next president of the USA. That Hillary Clinton is the She-Devil incarnate. What she needs is a good nuking from President Putin who definitely is not in the Ukraine, hell no. Keep America for the Americans. Build a wall along the Mexican border to keep out them scrounging narco Latinos out. Bomb somewhere, anywhere – now...'

"Er, thank you for sharing, Donald. Keep coming back. It works if you work it." ⊗

John Crace is The Guardian's parliamentary sketch writer and the writer of the Digested Reads column. He is also co-author, with Professor John Sutherland, of the Incomplete Shakespeare series, published by Doubleday

Write on Kew

Dozens of authors and acres of beauty. Enjoy more than 70 inspiring literary events. Book your place now.

KATE ADIE

ANTONY BEEVOR

MONTY DON

MARIAN KEYES

CAROL ANN DUFFY

Royal Botanic Gardens
Kew

22–25 September 2016

kew.org/writeonkew
Discounts for Friends of Kew
⊖ Kew Gardens ⇌ Kew Bridge

Proudly supported by **JMFinn&Co**

Whose name is on the frame?

45(03): 33/35 I DOI: 10.1177/0306422016670335

Artists in Turkey have been hiding their real identities with increasing frequency for more than a decade. **Kaya Genç** examines the innovative and subversive art works which this anonymity has allowed them to create

IF THE ATTEMPTED military coup on 15 July 2016 had succeeded and the curfews and martial law were imposed the following morning, the contemporary art field here would most likely have come to a halt for at least a year. But even before the coup, Turkey's contemporary artists had been using tactics of invisibility in order to keep themselves safe. In the last decade there has been a rise in the number of collectives who use pseudonyms while producing their works. Oda Projesi, Extramücadele, Hafriyat art group, -__-, iç-mihrak and Anti-pop are among the leading names who rose to fame in the 2000s. Members of art collectives put the names of their group before their own names, using them as cloaks beneath which they can more daringly produce art. Some known to be behind those names work in the advertising industry, others are academics and filmmakers: anonymity saves them from choosing between lucrative careers and radical experimentation that can get them into political trouble.

"Acting anonymously liberates you since it allows you to leave your identity behind," Amira Arzık, a curator with Istanbul's Pilot Gallery, told Index. "Watching the coup attempt on 15 July, I was reminded of the Turkish artist Burak Arıkan who reflected on how the artistic community would manage to stay in touch if all the communication channels were cut during a coup. Following the assassination of [the Turkish-Armenian journalist] Hrant Dink in 2007, a similarly traumatic event, an art collective was founded to allow the artistic community to be in touch. The anonymous 19 January Collective produced posters that combined activism and art, and that way connected people who were looking for answers regarding the assassination of Dink."

A legendary example of Turkish artistic collectives is 2/5 BZ. Founded in Istanbul in 1986, the multimedia project is known for using a combination of old films, zines, tapes and computer games in its video installations. The resulting patchwork always features a strong critique of Turkish capitalism and nationalism. From the gentrification of the cities to the killing of the country's minorities, 2/5 BZ had been on the front line of activism and art in Turkey and managed to move freely, thanks to its anonymity. In 2013 it became the leading collective at the environmental protests in Istanbul's Gezi Park.

"I was one of the people in Gezi Park, the very first day the uprising went huge →

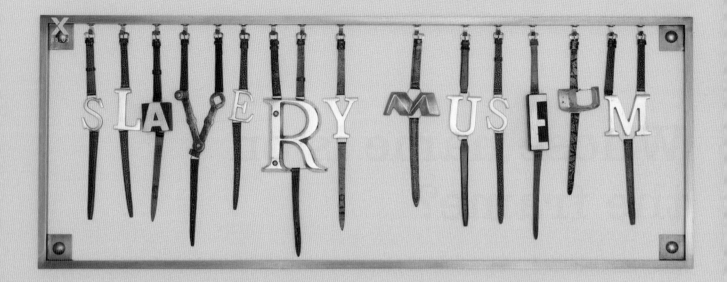

ABOVE: Slavery Museum, a work by artist Extramücadele

→ with millions of people around the country," 2/5 BZ wrote on the collective's Vimeo page. "During that police strike early in the morning, I was among a few people in that moment, who were being criminalised and terrorised because of their opponent positions. They wanted to bring me down, they targeted me, shot directly and consecutively towards me but could not succeed. However I fell and got injured. I have 22 titanium joints inside my shoulders. It has been two years now but the treatment and controls still goes on beside the court process."

An artist who followed in the footsteps of 2/5 BZ is Extramücadele, known as Extrastruggle in English. Extrastruggle's work is, according to international art brokers Sotheby's who sell it for thousands of pounds, "a moniker for a fictional graphic design company" and "a voice for the minorities in contemporary Turkey; the revolutionary, the Islamist, the intellectual and the rest". Two icons frequently used by Extrastruggle are burqa-wearing women (meant to symbolise Islam) and Mustafa Kemal Ataturk (the icon of the secularism of the Turkish Republic). Often these symbolic figures are juxtaposed in an effort to overcome cultural and political divides. Such works have become so popular, over the last decade, that Extrastruggle's cover was blown: nowadays, on his website (extramucadele.com) he uses his real name alongside the pseudonym.

Anti-pop, another Turkish anonymous artist who uses tactics of invisibility to escape the wrath of authorities, made a name via the website Anti-pop.com. There, images taken from Turkey's mainstream press are manipulated in order to show the discrimination of various groups in the country. Anti-pop's 2010 work Alevis in Turkey manipulates a Wikipedia map of Alawi groups in Turkey. Marking their existence in the country with the ominous red colour, it places location pins on the cities of Malatya and Maras, two cities where Alawi people were massacred by racists in 1970 and 1977.

"Traumas and ruptures in the social sphere result in art collectives," Arzık said. "Some use pseudonyms, thinking about the reactions to their works and using those names as precautions. At times anonymous art works produced on the streets, like those during the environmental protests at Gezi Park, can overshadow art works signed by the artists."

The use of pseudonyms has a long tradition in the Turkish art world. In Orhan Pamuk's 1999 novel My Name is Red, miniature artists Butterfly, Stork and Olive produce brilliant images and illustrate Islamic books while their real names are hidden from the reader. The convention is part of a tradition that accepts Ottoman artists and their freedom to work behind pen names. In Pamuk's novel, those artists are also murder suspects. It is their stylistic peculiarities as artists which give them away. The detective characters in My Name is Red can see their signatures in their art as well as in the murder of a fellow miniaturist; anonymity is liberating and lethal in the same instance.

In the poetic tradition of Ottoman literature, too, pseudonyms have long been a common feature. Authors would publish their divan poems, a tradition influenced by Persian use of symbolism, under pen names meant to best represent them: a poet known for the elegance of his rhetoric would be known as Zarifi (elegant), for example, and a more fanciful poet used the name Hayali (imaginary). According to conventions of divan poetry, the made-up name had to be used once in the final stanza of every work the poet produced. Of course, the authorities in the Ottoman palace knew who those poets were. When poets using pseudonyms were seen to be insulting the sultan, the writers were swiftly caught and in one terrifying example Nesimi (a poet known for his unorthodox religious beliefs) was skinned alive.

According to Turkish critic and art historian Süreyyya Evren, who recently edited the User's Manual 2.0, a book on the history of Turkish contemporary art, the increased use of pseudonyms among Turkish contemporary artists is linked to the phenomenon of the "precariat", a term used to refer to people without job security, as well as under political pressure.

People who suffer from precariousness, Evren explained to Index, were not members of the working class, nor were they real employees of companies. "They are always in between and are forced to embody a metaphor," Evren said. "These people who use such pseudonyms point to a new subjectivity. People manage their own name and turn into CEOs of their own brands. Members of the precariat are allowed to establish their own order." Like conscientious objectors who would burn their identity cards in a symbolic act to move out of the identity given to them by the state, contemporary artists use made-up names in order to produce new identities for themselves. "This way they create a new

balance between work and life," Evren said. This way an artist can fight against political power under a made-up name and work at a company in order to pay the bills. "It is about image management as well as a tactic of invisibility."

The propaganda design collective içmihrak is another group that uses such tactics. The collective aims at "designing high-quality propaganda material for anarchist/antiauthoritarian groups/individuals, completely free of charge", according to its website (icmihrak.blogspot.com.tr). In one poster içmihrak celebrates the new school year with a poster that features a hangman image, where the letters Q, W, X hang from a rope. The cryptic word below reads K_RT_E (Kurtce, or Kurdish), reflecting the battle Kurdish activ-

When poets using pseudonyms were seen to be insulting the sultan, the writers were swiftly caught and, in one terrifying example, a poet was skinned alive

ists long fought to be taught in state schools. "Dada Inside" reads another logo that copies the "Intel Inside" stickers, with "Semiotic Terrorism" inscribed underneath where the name of the processor normally is.

"Our fuel is fragments of official and popular culture (icons, iconic persons, slogans, sentimental sayings, modern and traditional values, universes of faith)," the group announced. "And the product of our initiative is a loud, uncontrollable laughter accompanied by stomach cramps that come from a sense of guilt – a state of euphoria." ⊗

Kaya Genç is based in Istanbul and is a contributing editor to Index on Censorship magazine. His new book Under the Shadow: Rage and Revolution in Modern Turkey (I.B. Tauris) is out now

ABOVE: A woman stands by a memorial to the victims of the Bastille Day attack in July 2016 in Nice. IS claimed responsibility for the deaths of 84 people on France's national holiday

CREDIT: Valery Hache/AFP/Getty Images

Spooks and sceptics

45(03): 36/39 | DOI: 10.1177/0306422016670336

Author and journalist **John Lloyd** argues that the public have to decide how much surveillance they are willing to accept and security services have to make sure they have public trust

PRIVACY, IN ANY sensible meaning of the word, is no longer an option for all but hermits in advanced democracies. The powers of security services around the world have been tightened after a rash of successful terrorist attacks this year and last, in the United States, France, Germany and Belgium. These were followed by warnings of more or worse to come. "Not if, but when," London Metropolitan Police Commissioner Bernard Hogan-Howe told BBC Radio 4's Today programme in early August.

It is a government's job to provide security, but it is increasingly the public's choice whether to accept the level of surveillance of phone calls and text messages that modern security services claim is necessary. If large-scale surveillance is accepted, as it presently is, with little dissent, it is the government's duty, and indeed a public duty to ensure that the intelligence agencies are explicitly part of the democratic order.

France, Germany, Canada and Australia all passed strong anti-terrorist laws last year, increasing the scope of surveillance and making arrests easier. Japan set up an anti-terrorist unit and strengthened its intelligence gathering capabilities. The UK will probably pass the Investigative Powers Act this year. These initiatives are not confined to democracies: both China, in 2015, and Russia, in 2016, also passed anti-terrorist legislation. The legislation was a first in China's case: both countries now require companies to store and release communications metadata.

Protests in Europe, particularly in Germany, against the US National Security Agency's surveillance methods after they were revealed by whistleblower Edward Snowden, have given way to a much more powerful desire from people for protection against terrorist attacks.

Polls in most Western countries record increased distrust of all Muslims. It has been Donald Trump's strongest card in his bid for the presidency fuelled by a more insistent fear of being assaulted, injured or murdered in a plane, a train or on the street. More protection means more surveillance. More surveillance means more of each individual's information being more accessible to more intelligence agencies.

The former US Undersecretary of Defense for Policy, Michelle Flournoy, recently wrote that opinion in European states, once sceptical or even contemptuous of the American war on terror and annoyed by the Edward Snowden and NSA revelations that the USA was spying on its allies "has swung dramatically toward security... in a Europe under regular attack by IS, more data collection and more information sharing, not less, appear to be the order of the day."

The Snowden-NSA revelations centred on the issue of privacy. They revealed that the NSA, and Britain's Government Communications Headquarters were capable of monitoring all communications traffic within their states, and abroad. The security agencies search the metadata – the data giving times, place, frequency, contacts rather than message content – for links between "persons of interest". Though a few parliamentarians and officials were aware of these programmes and investigative journalism in the USA had begun to prise out some details, the huge document dump from the NSA made the scale of the monitoring vividly clear.

A population made fearful and angry by constant terrorist attacks is one which becomes careless of democratic procedure and the rights of minorities

Privacy and its breaches have been at the core of arguments over the use of the internet since its early days. Battles were and still are waged over encryption, with academics, cypherpunks, who advocate for strong cryptography, and the Silicon Valley behemoths on one side, and the state in various guises on the other. Encryption is designed to keep messages and stored information private: the NSA, with other listening agencies, need to be able to break encryption to make sense of possibly dangerous linkages and conversations.

Academics and the cypherpunks, of whom Julian Assange was one before he founded the website Wikileaks, fought bitterly with the CIA for the right to use unbreakable encryption, a struggle later joined by some of the world's richest corporations, like Apple, Google and Facebook, all straining to convince their customers that they could protect their privacy. The journalist Misha Glenny has observed that "as governments and corporations amass ever more personal information about their citizens or clients, encryption is one of the few defences left to individuals to secure their privacy. It is also an invaluable instrument for those involved in criminal activity on the web". That includes the branch →

→ of criminality known as terrorism.

Snowden, with his closest allies, including the journalist Glen Greenwald and the filmmaker Laura Poitras, were militants for privacy and against the intrusion of the state. Greenwald, the most proactive of the group, regarded the semi-secret mass monitoring in the US and the UK as a fundamental betrayal, rendering governments illegitimate and bequeathing to journalism the necessary task not just of mainstream sceptical reporting but of aggressive unmasking of organisations that had forfeited any right to public trust. This is also a long-time belief of Julian Assange too.

The alarm that the contents of the published NSA files caused has proven for most people transient: the fear of more concentrated terrorism has been much more power-

A population made fearful and angry by constant terrorist attacks is one which becomes careless of democratic procedure

ful. The security services, always popular in the US and the UK, are even enjoying more support than usual in France, though support tempered by their failure to spot and stop the Paris attacks of 2015, and the Nice carnage and the murder of a Rouen priest in July 2016.

We can now assume the seriousness of the terrorists' ambitions; their possible acquisition of weapons of mass destruction; the attraction they have for some, especially the young, largely within Muslim communities; and their deliberate efforts to worsen relations between the settled and recent immigrant populations. As Philip Bobbitt, US author of Terror and Consent: the Wars for the Twenty-First Century, has written: "terrorism itself might become a threat to the legitimacy of those states that depend upon the consent of the governed". A failure to

stop or at least moderate terrorist attacks will make a democratic and civil society less democratic and civil.

A population made fearful and angry by constant terrorist attacks is one which becomes careless of democratic procedure and the rights of minorities. We do need the secret services, and we need them to be both in the front line against that threat, as well as fully and explicitly within the institutions of the democratic state. The fear that the security services can run names of individuals through their programmes without prior evidence of their danger can only be answered by trust in the agencies that they do not use the metadata examined for other than operational reasons.

Leaders of security services profess a strong attachment to the open society, to liberal freedoms and the rule of law. In his last speech before he retired Sir Iain Lobban, the former head of GCHQ, said: "We do what we do precisely to safeguard the kind of society that has a free press." He added: "We both seek the truth; and to get it, we both have to shine a light into dark and often dangerous places, places where we aren't exactly welcome." As we saw in Nice and Orlando, the perpetrators left little evidence that they were contemplating attacks. Security will never be wholly effective, but the agencies' claim is that the more links are made, the more likely it is that preventive action can be taken. That fact dictates strong and expert oversight of the agencies and clear sanctions within the agencies against any officers found to have misused the information gathered. Centres concerned with freedom of speech, the media, civil rights and civic engagement must see it as their duty to bring the security agencies into a conversation on how best to fulfill their responsibilities to protect, while ensuring that agencies take steps to make sure that their work is understood by citizens, whether secret or not.

Surveillance of our private messages must be scrupulously confined to that which is necessary for the provision of a secure society. A conversation of this kind has been limited so far, but the central position the intelligence agencies now occupy, the resources they demand and the power of their oversight requires a new settlement with the societies they protect. ⊗

John Lloyd is a contributing editor to the Financial Times and co-founded the Reuters Institute for the Study of Journalism. His book Journalism in an Age of Terror will be published by I.B. Tauris/Reuters Institute for the Study of Journalism later this year

PRIVACY AND ENCRYPTION: HOW I PROTECT MYSELF AND OTHERS

Jennifer Schulte is a human rights researcher and social scientist with over a decade of experience. She researches sexual violence, surveillance and censorship in Africa. Feeling threatened by the ultra-conservative Salafists in Egypt in 2012, she left for London, then Iceland where she met someone working with Wikileaks. They told her to get an XMPP account for secure messaging. She soon began encrypting her communications. Below, she talks about why.

How do you protect your digital privacy?
If I'm having a private meeting, we probably won't bring our phones, and we'll talk in a park. I rely on a mix of analogue and digital tactics; varying routines, keeping people on a need-to-know basis, passing messages through trusted third parties, not writing everything down until it's safe, not digitising field notes until you are out of a country, not using smart phones for calls and texts. And I always keep in mind that some countries have laws against using strong encryption software.

Why did you start to learn about strict information security practices?
Anyone who works on gender-based violence knows that privacy can save lives. It's absolutely required to protect the people we serve. If I inadvertently leak information because I can't handle my digital security, then I can put lives at risk. At a training session I gave recently in eastern Europe, I was not surprised to hear that safe houses in the country do not allow smartphones. They knew that GPS and other technologies have introduced new risks. Phones infected with spyware can give you away to someone who is trying to hunt and kill you.

Do you think privacy is dead?
If you say privacy is dead, whose privacy are you talking about? Activists in Johannesburg need privacy in order to organise their protests. A lot of human rights organising in Ethiopia explicitly happens away from phones and the internet because of longstanding awareness of mass and targeted surveillance by an authoritarian state. When I was working in the camps on the Somali border, the government insisted that I take what they called a "colleague", who was a spy, into my human rights interviews with Somali refugee girls. I passed out large sheets of paper with coloured markers and had the girls draw for an hour, a research method called safety-mapping and storytelling. The girls drew in almost complete silence while the spy was in the room. After an hour, the spy seemed to lose interest, maybe she thought that I was doing an art project. As soon as she left the room, the girls started talking. The floodgates opened up about abductions and rapes in the hills.

As told to Bethany Horne

"I have a name"

45(03): 40/41 | DOI: 10.1177/0306422016670338

After the brutal murders of other writers in his country, Bangladeshi blogger **Ananya Azad** began to receive death threats – so he fled to Germany. He explains why he chose not to write anonymously

I HAVE A NAME. I am not anonymous. But what if I didn't have a name? What if I could enjoy the luxury of being safe at home in Bangladesh, and not far away in Germany?

I could have distanced myself from my identity, adopted a pseudonym and continued to write in Bangladesh. Had I done so, my family wouldn't have to spend each moment in fear and anxiety. My sister wouldn't have to wake up from nightmares about rape threats. But I am not anonymous. I carry my name and history with me. And so the possibility of an unnatural death haunts me.

Since 2013, my name has surfaced on multiple "hit lists" targeting Bangladeshi bloggers and other activists. I still regularly receive death threats from religious extremists on Facebook and other social media. One simply told me, "It's your turn now."

My words often create problems for others. I see myself as writing for the freedom of various groups, for the rights of oppressed communities, for women, for the sexually marginalised. In my debut book Chastity Versus Polygamy, I addressed the patriarchal notion of purity that is assigned to women's sexuality; this was considered controversial and it enraged many.

I strongly believe that all human beings possess an equal right to express themselves, to assert their ideas and to be recognised for who they are and what they want to be. When the identity of the writer is out in the open, along with a certain level of insecurity comes a burden of responsibility that commits the writer to his or her words. This is why anonymity never appealed to me. I had faith in the democratic setup of my country, Bangladesh. But the state failed to uphold our freedom by suggesting we should stop writing, rather than that terrorism should stop. So I left.

Anonymous bloggers and activists in Bangladesh come from all parts of the

LEFT: Bangladeshi blogger Ananya Azad in his apartment in Hamburg, Germany, in July 2015, where he currently lives in exile after receiving death threats from Islamists for his blogging

ideological spectrum. They include religious radicals, communists, liberals. Unfortunately, certain sections of this anonymous community aim to create chaos, rather than a constructive democratic debate. A number of them publish hate speech, or post videos which are meant to incite violence.

Generally, however, the bloggers are on the receiving end of aggression. Sometimes, even anonymity is no protection. Those who would silence them are often incredibly adept at technological espionage, and can all too easily crack their identities. In March 2015, anonymous atheist blogger Washiqur Rahman Babu was traced and killed in broad daylight outside his residence. Even I didn't know his identity at the time.

In the face of threats, therefore, going anonymous is hardly a foolproof solution.

When a writer's identity is out in the open, they have a burden of responsibility that commits them to their words

However, it may not always be feasible to declare one's identity under dire circumstances, which is the case in many places across the world right now. Anonymity might turn to be one of the necessary shields in the larger, longer battle for free speech. ⊗

Ananya Azad, a Bangladeshi writer and blogger, is currently in exile in Germany. His father, author Humayun Azad, was the victim of assassination attempts, and later died in mysterious circumstances

The smear factor

45(03): 42/43 | DOI: 10.1177/0306422016670339

Rupert Myers looks at the power of anonymous allegations to damage the lives and careers of politicians

ABOVE: An anonymous smear about former UK Prime Minister David Cameron's sparked a variety of cartoons and this piñata carried by protesters in London in April 2016

IN DONALD TRUMP'S ongoing campaign to be president of the USA, he has often repeated the claim that his rival Hillary Clinton began the so-called "birther" conspiracy. It harks back to spring 2008. Desperate for their candidate to win the Democratic nomination over Barack Obama, some of Clinton's supporters began circulating an anonymous email, questioning whether Obama was born in the USA, and thus disputing his eligibility to be president.

It's the conspiracy theory that has never gone away – even after Obama produced his birth certificate to show he was born in Hawaii. A recent NBC News poll claimed that 72% of registered Republican voters still doubt President Obama's citizenship.

Trump – despite originally questioning the birth certificate himself – has, during his own campaign, taken to suggesting Clinton herself started the rumour. It's a smear that has been difficult for the Clinton campaign to kill off, because of the anonymous nature of the initial claim.

UK politicians have suffered a similar fate

CREDIT Mark Kerrison / Alamy

from anonymous allegations. A single anonymous source to David Cameron's unofficial biographers dented the then prime minister's reputation in 2015 with the allegation that he had engaged in an ill-judged undergraduate drinking society ritual with the head of a dead pig. In the ensuing days and weeks after the story broke, few if any seemed to care whether the story was in fact true. A survey by UK polling company YouGov found that 66% of people believed the claim, despite not knowing the identity of the single source. Some 30% considered the allegation important to the question of the prime minister's capacity to lead. That's just under 20 million people, or around 10 times the gap in the popular vote between the Conservative and Labour parties at the last general election.

Anonymous smears have been proven to carry weight with the public, with percentages of the population believing them often significantly greater than the margins of political victory. In a climate when political rallies boo journalists, and activists can share posts on Facebook that are misleading or inaccurate, the potential reach and harm of a political smear is enormous. When the chances of detection are so slim, and the potential gains so great, why wouldn't some political campaigns set out to smear their opponents? The widespread availability of secure technology means that it may be impossible to track the source of a smear, or then to do anything about it. Legal action against anonymous trolls is likely to be extremely costly and ineffective as a means of deterrence.

Anonymous accounts can be used to amend Wikipedia, the first place many online researchers turn. They can contact jurors and witnesses, or even fabricate allegations online which jurors may stumble upon. None of this is beyond the capacity of criminals seeking to avoid conviction. The deliberations of juries are secret, and methods like this are necessarily going to be covert. A 2014 survey of US District Court Judges

found that 7% had caught jurors doing such research, which suggests that the total numbers are far higher.

In the UK, politician Grant Schapps was caught out in 2015 after a series of amends were made to his Wikipedia page to remove embarrassing stories. Wikipedia banned the anonymous account involved, stating concerns that it was managed by Schapps or one of his team. The same account had also toyed with the pages of other politicians.

Anonymous disinformation and smears can reduce the credibility of politicians in a democracy. And the globalised social media environment adds to the reach of those smears, which travel at speed over borders. The tools of a modern free and open society

Anonymous accounts can be used to contact jurors and witnesses, even fabricate allegations

can be used against it by the state and other players. There are reports that the Kremlin is directly involved in the widespread dissemination of propaganda via online trolls. Trump gains vocal support online from anonymous bots. The Mexican and Turkish governments have also been accused of having armies of bots on social media. At best, these add to the general level of noise and make individuals, and the truth, harder to hear. At worst these methods can channel hatred, lies and abuse. There are many legitimate reasons for anonymity, but the tools we are using to grant it are blunt, obviously open to manipulation, and a threat to the quality of our free speech. Worse, they may have a serious negative impact upon our justice systems, and our democratic processes. ⊗

Rupert Myers is the political editor for GQ Magazine in the UK

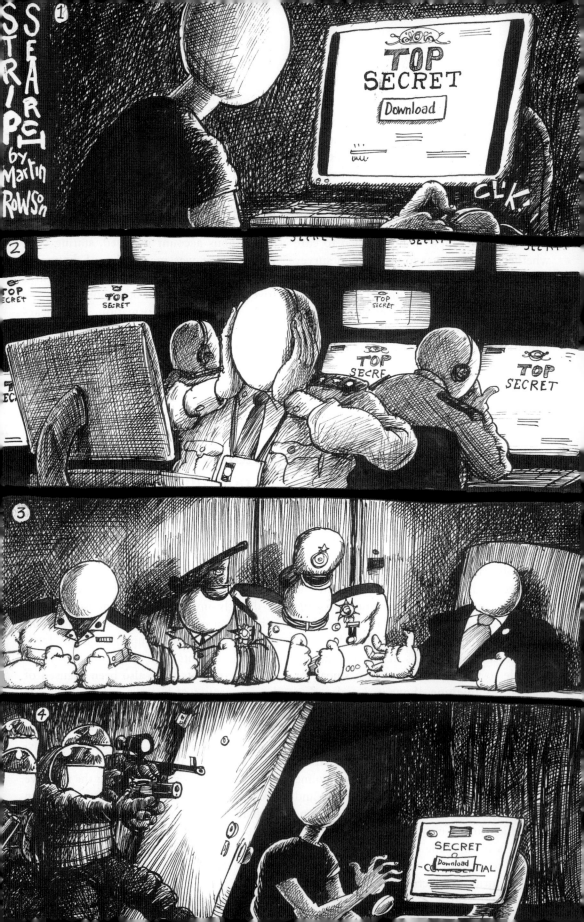

Signing off

45(03): 46/47 | DOI: 10.1177/0306422016670341

Writing under a pen name has been a feature of literary history, ranging from the Brontë sisters to Søren Kierkegaard, says **Julian Baggini**

THE CONCEALMENT OF identity has two contrasting faces. There is the creative, exploratory aspect of the actor's mask or the child's role-playing but there is also the sinister disguise of the assassin or the fearful, furtive dissimulation of the persecuted fugitive.

Unfortunately, there are still many writers around the world who adopt pseudonyms for negative rather than positive reasons, the most obvious of these being self-preservation. Historically, the biggest threat has been religious persecution, which is why even as late as 1770, the atheist Franco-German thinker Paul-Henri Thiry, Baron d'Holbach, published his The System of Nature under the name of Jean-Baptiste de Mirabaud, a man who had been dead for 10 years.

Nowadays, political heresy is a more common motivation for preserving an author's anonymity, but we should remember that when the church wielded great power, theocratic dissent was political dissent, as it remains in several Islamic countries today. Less has changed than we might hope.

The other major historical motivation to adopt a pseudonym is to give voice to those who could not publish under their real identities, most notably women. That is why in the 19th century the Brontë sisters wrote under the names of Currer (Charlotte), Ellis (Emily) and Acton (Anne) Bell. Although women's rights have come a long way since then, it is worth noting that women can still not be sure of being taken as seriously as men, which is why the author of Harry Potter adopted the semi-pseudonym of JK Rowling, after being advised boys would not want to read a book written by a Joanne.

It should be a minimum aspiration that we live in a world where no one is forced to adopt a pseudonym for the sake of self-preservation or to get a hearing. If we achieved this, however, that would not render the pseudonym redundant or harmless.

In a free society, anonymity ceases to be a way to protect authors and instead becomes a way of making it easier to harm their enemies. The internet has opened up a whole new set of problems for those who naively believe that the only deep problem of free speech is its suppression. We have seen many people use the opportunities to hide their identities online to intimidate, abuse and defame. It is difficult to know how to deal with this without introducing dangerous curbs on freedom of expression, but it is an issue we cannot just ignore.

There are therefore two types of "dark pseudonymity": that which protects against harm and that which enables the infliction of harm. But even in an open society, there are uses of the defensive variety. Writers who have no fear of persecution may still dread the prospect of public exposure and scrutiny. Privacy is hard to defend when almost everyone has a smartphone and there are no end of websites, newspapers and magazines all too eager to report almost any detail of a celebrity's life.

This is not entirely new of course. For Charles Dodgson, the name Lewis Carroll enabled him to continue as an Oxford scholar without the distraction of his literary fame and also to preserve some privacy. Today, however, freedom from intrusion is even harder to protect. So although the real person who writes under the name of Elena Ferrante can be thankful that her sex is no longer a barrier to publication, it is understandable that she (or he) still prefers to keep her identity a secret to enable her to live a private life. Such cases illustrate how enabling freedom of speech can inhibit the freedom of people to live private lives, another dilemma that naive defenders of free speech without qualification are wrong to dismiss.

There are, however, some uses of pseudonyms that are entirely positive. Rowling adopted the nom de plume Robert Galbraith for her adult crime novels "to work without hype or expectation and to receive totally unvarnished feedback." Her pen name enabled her to remove the weight of expectation and prejudice and to offer her work as though she were a literary debutante.

Eric Blair's reasons for writing as George Orwell are less clear. In part it seemed it enabled him to avoid the baggage his birth name had acquired as that of a mediocre, jobbing hack. It has also been suggested that he simply didn't want to embarrass his respectable parents with the stories of his slumming it in Down and Out in London and Paris.

But perhaps the greatest use of the pseudonym is not to enable you to write freely as yourself, but to become another. That was the motivation behind Søren Kierkegaard's prodigious pseudonymous output. Anonymity was not the issue here: everyone in Copenhagen knew who was behind the work of the likes of Johannes de Silentio, Constantine Constantius, Hilarius Bookbinder and Anti-Climacus, hardly names designed to disguise their artifice.

For Kierkegaard, adopting a pseudonym was borrowing an identity, a world view. It

was a way to write about a way of seeing the world from the inside, from a perspective that he himself did not endorse. It might be called an exercise in intellectual empathy, getting a sense not only of how others feel but how they think. This enterprise is even more relevant today, when identities have become freer and more fluid. Playing with different perspectives is no longer just a way of getting out of ourselves but having the

ABOVE: JK Rowling at an event to discuss her books written under the pseudonym Robert Galbraith

We have seen many people use the opportunities to hide their identities online to intimidate

freedom to explore the diversities contained within ourselves.

Kierkegaard thus represents the opposite end of a spectrum. At its worst, a pseudonym is a desperate necessity, the only means of writing as yourself. At its best, it is a freely chosen way of writing as another or extending oneself. The world views that determine which form of pseudonym prevails are fundamentally opposed in values. In one, the minds of others are to be controlled and suppressed, while in the other they are seen as places to be explored with openness and interest. ⊗

Julian Baggini is a member of the Index editorial board and author of Freedom Regained: The Possibility of Free Will (Granta)

The Snowden effect

45(03): 48/50 I DOI: 10.1177/0306422016670343

Most people, despite Edward Snowden's revelations, are still fairly apathetic about protecting their online privacy. But if it's easier to do, will we adopt methods to guard our online selves? **Charlie Smith** from anti-censorship campaigners Great Fire gives his advice

IT'S BEEN MORE than three years since Edward Snowden revealed the incredible scale of mass surveillance. Yet, even as his story gets the Oliver Stone treatment in a new Hollywood movie, the general public has still failed to adopt privacy-enhancing tools en masse.

Snowden himself predicted this when he stepped out of the shadows and invited reporters from The Guardian newspaper into his Hong Kong hotel room in June 2013.

"I know the media likes to personalise political debates, and I know the government will demonise me," Snowden told The Guardian at the time. "I really want the focus to be on these documents and the debate which I hope this will trigger among citizens around the globe about what kind of world we want to live in."

His analysis was correct. Many media outlets have focused on Snowden, the person, instead of the issues surrounding mass surveillance. The effort to downplay the revelations has arguably proven effective as most individuals have shrugged off the idea that the authorities are monitoring their communications. Those that are aware of mass surveillance are mostly nonchalant. Most do not want to engage in a debate because they believe they "have nothing to hide" in the first place.

Is this really the world that people want to live in? Probably not. Efforts have been made to explain the National Security Agency leaks in simple language. When Edward Snowden was interviewed by TV presenter John Oliver for his US show Last Week Tonight in April 2015, they discussed how people are mostly concerned whether or not the government is collecting photos of their private parts. (They are, said Snowden. Not as a particular "Dick Pic Program", but because they get swept up with bulk collection of online activity.) Yet even this has failed to drive adoption of privacy-enhancing tools. At the heart of the matter is habit. Most people are too lazy to change their current routines when it comes to protecting their privacy. Companies such as Facebook make it difficult for users to take matters into their own hands by complicating and changing the privacy settings.

Snowden's actions mobilised and energised the developers of privacy-enhancing tools. A plethora of choices now exist for those who want to protect their privacy. There are so many choices that the internet freedom community itself is at times guilty of debating the merits of individual tools instead of encouraging adoption.

This past year, however, saw one exceptional and largely unheralded development

in this space. Non-profit software group Open Whisper Systems has come to the forefront to, as their website states, "advance the state of the art for secure communication, while simultaneously making it easy for everyone to use". They developed the encrypted call and messaging app Signal, which was released at the end of 2015 and was publicly praised by fanboy Snowden. "I use Signal every day. #notesfortheFBI (Spoiler: they already know)," Snowden tweeted last November, and Signal received an uptick in users amid the surrounding publicity.

But perhaps the greatest development in pushing everybody towards secure and encrypted communication was when OWS launched a partnership to incorporate their technology into the globally popular WhatsApp chat app. In April, hundreds of millions of people woke up to find out the

People are mostly concerned whether or not the government is collecting photos of their private parts

messages they were sending to their family and friends would be encrypted. Many would come to understand that this would mean that their communications would be invisible to the prying eyes of the NSA and their partners around the world. What was the price for this newfound privacy? Absolutely nothing. Users were informed of the changes when they logged on to WhatsApp. No settings had to be changed. No new app had to be downloaded.

What's more, there has been a domino effect after the OWS integration. →

ABOVE: Joseph Gordon-Levitt stars in new film Snowden

→ Consumers have been putting pressure on other messaging and communications platforms to implement end-to-end encryption for their services. The positive end result is that we should expect to see more communications apps implement end-to-end encryption by default.

The internet freedom community is building off of this momentum and needs to take advantage of arguably unrelated market conditions to expand private communications beyond the community of activists and others who need to protect their privacy. Most importantly, this community needs to seek out collaborative partnerships like the one between OWS and WhatsApp. It also needs to recognise that most people are not interested in using new apps and tools. Instead, the focus should be on integrating privacy,

It needs to recognise that most people are not interested in using new apps or tools

secure communications and encryption into the world's most popular communications platforms.

Recent leaks have highlighted the importance of encrypting email. In July, WikiLeaks released almost 20,000 emails from the US Democratic National Committee, revealing that some delegates were undermining Senator Bernie Sanders in his bid to be the party's presidential candidate. If Sanders runs for office again in four years' time, it is unlikely that the DNC will conspire against him in normal, written, plain-text email communications.

Fully encrypted email services do exist but there is a WhatsApp-like opportunity to suddenly put the power of encrypted email into the hands of more than one billion Gmail users and companies that use Gmail to power their work email. The Mailvelope app seamlessly integrates with Gmail to provide a simple yet secure solution for encrypted messages within the Gmail interface itself. While Mailvelope has yet to formally strike a deal with Google, it is certainly not inconceivable that consumers demand that Gmail offer an integrated solution for encryption. For Google, this will be about meeting consumer demand. And for the internet freedom community, this is about making it is as easy as possible for a great number of users to start encrypting email.

Geographical restrictions on the viewing of online content have brought virtual private network usage to the forefront. VPNs help you browse the internet more anonymously by routing your traffic through a server in a different location or country, and are now commonly used to circumvent geographical restrictions on the viewing of content.

Some companies have recently cracked down on the use of VPNs to circumvent content-viewing restrictions, including movie-streaming site Netflix, which says it will step up enforcement against subscribers who use VPNs to access localised content from different countries.

Yet the adoption of tools to circumvent these restrictions has had the added benefit of masking the internet traffic of many people. This is a great market opportunity for privacy advocates. Increased demand for VPNs will help to drive down prices. Increased competition will also help to improve quality, making them easy to purchase and install on as many devices as possible, allowing greater privacy to proliferate.

As privacy enhancing tools start to move mainstream, our online habits will also change. By taking back control of our privacy, free expression of ideas and opinions will proliferate, without the fear of retribution. ⊗

Charlie Smith is a pseudonym. A winner of an Index on Censorship Freedom of Expression award in 2016, he is one of the co-founders of GreatFire.org

Leave no trace

45(03): 51/53 I DOI: 10.1177/0306422016670344

Staying truly anonymous online is not easy when trackers from ad builders to governments may be trying to read your every keystroke. **Mark Frary** looks at some of the tactics you can use to remain safer or invisible when browsing

Securing your connection

Activists in countries where the web is heavily censored and internet traffic is closely monitored know that using a virtual private network or VPN is essential for remaining invisible.

A VPN is like a pair of curtains on a house: people know you are in but cannot see what you are doing. This is achieved by creating an encrypted tunnel via a private host, often in another country, through which your internet data flows. This means that anyone monitoring web traffic to find out persons of interest is unable to do so. However, the very fact that you are using a VPN may raise eyebrows.

An increasing number of VPNs promise truly anonymous access and do not log any of your activity, such as ExpressVPN (.expressvpn.com) and Anonymizer (anonymizer.com). However, access to some VPN providers is blocked in some countries and their accessibility is always changeable.

Know your onions

One of the internet's strengths is also one of its weaknesses, at least as far as privacy is concerned. Traffic passes over the internet in data packets, each of which may take a different route between sender and recipient, hopping between computer nodes along the way. This makes the network resilient to

physical attack – since there is no fixed connection between the endpoints – but also helps to identify the sender. Packets contain information on both the sender's and recipient's IP address so if you need anonymity, this is a fatal flaw.

"Onion" routing offers more privacy. In this, data packets are wrapped in layers of encryption, similar to the layers of an onion. At each node, a layer of encryption is removed, revealing where the packet is to go next, the benefit being that the node only knows the address details of the preceding and succeeding nodes and not the entire chain.

Using onion routing is not as complicated as it may sound. In the mid-1990s, US naval researchers created a browser called TOR, short for The Onion Routing project, based on the concept and offered it to anyone under a free licence.

Accessing the dark web with the Tor browser (torproject.org) is a powerful method of hiding identity but is not foolproof. There are a number of documented techniques for exploiting weaknesses and some people believe that some security agencies use these to monitor traffic.

Put the trackers off your scent

Every time you visit a popular website, traces of your activity are carefully collected →

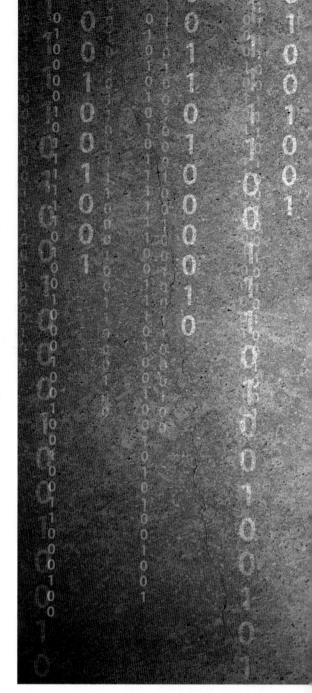

→ and sifted, often by snippets of code that come from other parts of the web. A browser add-on called Ghostery (ghostery.com) can show you just how prevalent this is. Firing up Ghostery on a recent visit to The Los Angeles Times website turned up 102 snippets of code designed to track web activity, ranging from well-known names such as Facebook and Google but also lesser known names such as Audience Science and Criteo.

While some of this tracking has legitimate uses, such as to personalise what you see on a site or to tailor the ads that appear, some trackers, particularly in countries where there are lax or no rules about such things, are working hard to identify you.

The problem is that trackers can work out who you are by jigsaw identification. Imagine you have visited a few places on the web, including reading an online article in a banned publication and then flicking

The very fact that you are using a VPN may raise eyebrows

through a controversial discussion forum. A third-party tracker used for serving ads can now learn about this behaviour. If you then subsequently log into another site, such as a social network, that includes your identity, this information can suddenly be linked together. Open-source browser extensions such as Disconnect (disconnect.me) offer a way to disable such trackers.

Use the secure web

A growing number of popular websites force visitors to connect to them securely. You can tell which ones because their addresses begin with https rather than http. Using https means that the website you are visiting will be authenticated and that your communications with the site are encrypted, stopping so-called man-in-the-middle attacks – where a malicious person sits between two people

who believe they are communicating directly with each other and alters what is being communicated. Google, as well as using https for both Gmail and search, is also encouraging other websites to adopt it by boosting such sites up the search rankings.

Rather than remembering to check you are using https all the time, some people employ a browser extension created by the Electronic Frontier Foundation and the Tor Project called HTTPS Everywhere (eff.org/ https-everywhere) to do it for them. It is available for Chrome, Firefox and Opera and forces browsers to user https versions of sites where available.

Hide your fingerprints

Traditional identification methods on the web rely on things like IP addresses and cookies, but some organisations employ far more sophisticated techniques, such as browser fingerprinting. When you visit a site, the browser may share information on your default language and any add-ons and fonts you have installed. This may sound innocuous, but this combination of settings may be unique to you and, while not letting others know who you are, can be used to associate your web history with your browser's fingerprint. You can see how poorly you are protected by visiting panopticlick.eff.org.

One way to try to avoid this is to use a commonly used browser set-up, such as Chrome running on Windows 10 and only common add-ins activated and the default range of fonts. Turning off Javascript can also help but also makes many sites unusable. You can also install the EFF's Privacy Badger browser add-on to thwart invisible trackers. ⊗

Mark Frary is a journalist and co-author of You Call This The Future?: The Greatest Inventions Sci-Fi Imagined and Science Promised (Chicago Review Press, 2008)

ABOVE: An increasing number of VPNs allows users completely anonymous access and avoids having their activity logged

Goodbye to
the byline

45(03): 54/55 I DOI: 10.1177/0306422016670345

Edward Lucas, senior editor at The Economist, on why the publication doesn't put its writers' names on stories

IN AN AGE that celebrates personality, anonymity is a distinctive feature of our journalism (mystique for fans, a marketing gimmick if you want to be cynical). It gives an air of authority and a sense of collective endeavour to what we write. It makes it hard for critics to dismiss an Economist article as merely the work of a disgruntled or ignorant journalist: everything has the same imprimatur. The authority comes from the brand, not the individual journalist. This has practical uses. It protects individual correspondents from reprisals – when writing about people or regimes who take criticism personally.

find The Economist to their taste. Even if our star writers, the columnists who write Bagehot, Banyan, Bello, Charlemagne, Free Exchange, Lexington and Schumpeter, are away or indisposed, their places can be seamlessly taken by colleagues. Nobody is irreplaceable and we all know it.

You can still become famous as an Economist writer. You can write books. You can broadcast and pontificate, chair conferences, give speeches, moonlight at a think-tank (or all of the above). Our press office, tasked with telling the world that we are not as dull as our name suggests, tries hard to get the authors of our most provocative and impor-

LEFT: Recent covers of The Economist

Anonymity filters out the egomaniacs so often found in other reaches of journalism

Anonymity saves time and hassle. Creating a byline that allocated credit fairly among half a dozen people who may have contributed to the article would be cumbersome (and of little interest to the readers). Anonymity removes the problem and spurs collaboration. You don't barge in front in the hope of a star billing. You lean in, in the knowledge that the people who matter most – your colleagues and bosses – will be keenly aware of what you contribute.

But it also reflects the way we write. Articles are conceived, reported (sometimes in half-a-dozen places) written, rewritten, rewritten again, fact-checked, copy-edited, and tweaked. They may stem from an idea by one author, be mostly written by a second, owe their polish to a third and their memorable sparkle to a fourth.

Anonymity filters out the egomaniacs so often found in other reaches of journalism. They will head for the bright lights of television, or for the kind of written media which offers large picture bylines. They will not

tant articles on to television and radio. Our online-only pieces, which are mostly less heavily edited and more personal, usually have initials: it helps the reader to connect articles to others by the same writers – even without knowing who they actually are. But in the print edition, anonymity reigns unchallenged.

It may seem a quaint throwback, or even an affectation. But it works. Our circulation is strong and our profits healthy; we have no difficulty in hiring or keeping talented staff. Anonymity was ubiquitous in journalism when we published our first edition in 1843: putting your name on an article was seen as showing off. Admittedly it is rare now: in the UK, only Private Eye follows the same practice. But few if any of the 100-plus staffers and stringers who now write for the paper (never, ever a "magazine") would want it any other way. It is a blessing, not a curse. ⊗

Edward Lucas is a senior editor at The Economist

CREDIT: Jonathan Wiggs / The Boston Globe via Getty Images

What's your emergency?

45(03): 56/59 I DOI: 10.1177/0306422016670346

What happens when online threats move into the real world, asks
Jason DaPonte, as he looks at the rise of potentially dangerous hoaxes

professor of law at the New York Law School and expert in cyber-harassment told Index. A common reaction has been to tell people receiving online threats that they should stop using social media. The police, said Waldman, often struggle to know how to handle this growing problem. "There are laws out there, but law enforcement agencies are sometimes just stretched too thin."

Brian Krebs, the editor of the tech security blog Krebs on Security, was one of the first journalists to be "swatted" in 2013. His home address in the US state of Virginia was obtained, an anonymous call was made, and heavily armed police were sent to his house to bust a hostage situation that didn't exist. Since then a variation of the trick has arrived in the UK: Justine Roberts, founder of online parenting community Mumsnet, also had armed police turn up at her house in the middle of the night in 2015, after reports that a gunman was on the loose there. Roberts was away at the time, but said her au pair woke with a start when police burst in. She became the victim of hackers, who had brought down the Mumsnet website.

In the wake of the murder of British MP Jo Cox in June 2016, a number of female MPs who have been victims of online threats have been cautioned by police to increase their security. Scottish MP Nicola McGarry worries about how these attacks could silence political participation. A spokesperson for McGarry told Index, "This strikes at the heart of the challenge facing our politics and democracy. We already face a gulf in the equal representation of women, people living with disabilities and LGBT people in our democracy. People will be driven away from participating in politics as long as this savage side of the internet is left unchallenged."

Swatting attacks, however, are difficult to prevent because once a call to the emergency services is made, authorities have little choice but to respond. The danger is, although most victims immediately co-operate and are thus not harmed, children or others in the →

LEFT: Victims of swatting attacks are having their homes raided by police Swat teams after online trolls place hoax emergency calls

IMAGINE AN ARMED Special Weapons and Tactics team surrounding your home following a hoax call that an emergency crime situation is under way. Hollywood is all too familiar with this trick, known as "swatting". Entertainers including Tom Cruise, Justin Bieber and the Kardashian family have all been reported victims of an anonymous tip-off to the police. Writers, gamers and members of the public have also been targeted. Some writers have taken it as a warning, a clear indication that they are being watched and should watch their step.

"Don't just tell [victims] to turn off their computers," Ari Ezra Waldman, associate

||||||||||||||||||||||||||||||||||||||||||||||||||||||||||||||||||||||||||||||||||||||||||||||||||||||||||||||||||||||||||

YAKETY YAK
(DON'T HATE BACK)

···

SEAN VANNATA looks at how an anonymous social network was banned on some US university campuses

A social media app that allowed users to trade thoughts while remaining unidentified has narrowed its idea of complete anonymity after complaints of cyberbullying. Yik Yak, which launched in the USA in 2013 and became popular across college campuses, introduced mandatory profiles for users in July this year.

The social network offers students in the same area the ability to talk among themselves, contributing comments, known as "Yaks", to a single thread. Yet, unlike on Twitter or Facebook, posts could not be traced to a single user.

Many argued that this complete anonymity encouraged cyber bullying and hate speech. In November 2014, during the peak of Yik

Yak's popularity, Utica College in New York blocked the app on university servers after multiple complaints from students. A number of other schools have also banned it.

A group of African American students at the University of Pittsburgh released a video of themselves reading racist Yaks aloud. "Hate black people more and more everyday [...] get a job, get off the street, and stop acting like a bunch of zoo creatures," read one. A student from Western Washington University is currently awaiting trial for malicious harassment, relating to alleged posts on the network.

Yik Yak has slowly moved away from total anonymity by introducing direct messaging, the ability to post pictures, and usernames. The new profiles do not require a real name or picture, but users can now view a profile behind a Yak. From July 2015 it has required users to verify their accounts with a phone number. It has also employed geofencing to control who can use it. Yik Yak's website says, "We disable Yik Yak near middle and high schools to combat bullying."

→ targeted home or business who may not know what's happening could get caught in the middle, or an item being carried by the homeowner could be mistaken for a weapon and police may respond accordingly. YouTube videos of the attacks – which have been captured after hackers take control of users' webcams – have shown gamers wearing headphones, not hearing the authorities approaching and getting wrestled to the ground at their computers after the police break in.

Doxxing is the main practice that leads to swatting attacks (see Doxxed in Volume 44, 3/2015). This is the disclosure of the personal details (including home address) of individuals so they can be targeted with physical threats and harm. It is a widespread practice carried out by malicious hackers that have

often released the documents (aka "docs" or "dox") that show where their enemies live. Doxxing is not technically illegal, though hacking to get people's personal information is, as is inciting violence against an individual. In July, Mir Islam, a 22-year-old from New York, was convicted of cybercrime (along with other charges) and sentenced to a two-year prison term. He was part of an anonymous syndicate which was behind the swatting attack on the Krebs' house, and which also published online the personal details of celebrities and officials, including First Lady Michelle Obama.

"Perpetrators of these hoaxes purposely use our emergency responders to harm their victims," said US Congresswoman Katherine Clark (D-MA) in November 2015 when she introduced a House bill to tighten US laws on swatting. Currently, US federal law prohibits bomb or terrorist-attack hoax calls but not the false reporting of other emergency situations. The new bill aims to close this loophole. "These false reports are dangerous and costly, and have resulted in serious injury to victims and law enforcement. It is time to update our laws to appropriately address this crime," said Clark, who, just a few months after speaking out, herself became a victim of a swatting attack.

Right-wing free speech activist, author and lawyer Mike Cernovitch from Los Angeles, claims to have suffered swatting threats and attacks that have forced him to stay in hotels to avoid being home when attacks might come. He told Index: "I'm generally against more federal laws but … the feds have far more resources than local resources do to prosecute swatting."

Cernovitch claimed he was swatted because he was embroiled in the "GamerGate" controversy in 2014 where people on both sides of a debate on sexism in the gaming industry suffered cyber harassment because of their opinions. He told Index his feelings about general online threats are different to his feelings about swatting and that there is a need for stronger laws against swatting. "Online threats simply aren't credible and police have learned that nothing happens when they investigate. I have never heard of anyone having a death threat they get on the internet carried out on them. The recipients shouldn't take them seriously," he said.

Staff at HeartMob, a platform against online harassment that launched in January in New York, disagree. Their team takes threats very seriously – those that users report on their site and those that their staff will receive as a result. Before launching, they put a multi-point safety plan in place. This included: obscuring all personal information about their five members of staff and their families to avoid them being doxxed, as well as a number of physical measures including added security at their office, a plan for a swatting attack, and carrying pepper spray with them.

"We received death threats because we were launching a project to protect people harassed online. They tried to silence us and tried to make the project too risky to do," Emily May, the chief executive of the company behind the project, told Index.

Law enforcement is often seen to be slow to respond to the online threats like those made to Hollaback, the company behind HeartMob, because the threats aren't seen to be "actual and specific" or "real" because they occur online. "Police need to get with the times," May said.

Swatting and doxxing are normally carried out using online anonymity tools that are designed to protect people online; which unfortunately means that it can be incredibly

Webcams have shown gamers getting wrestled to the ground after the police break in

difficult to trace and prosecute them especially because the investigations often have to cross national borders. A Canadian teenager, known online under the screen-name Obnoxious, was prosecuted in July 2015 for serial swatting, including a reported eight-hour video "marathon" of him swatting victims' homes; the investigation by Canadian and US police had taken over a year.

"The national/international nature of some of these crimes means that we need a national or international approach. It's not uncommon for the FBI to work to identify criminals who try to hide [between jurisdictions]," Waldman told Index. "It wouldn't be hard, we have the technology to do it – we can't just rely on a local police department that deals with all the local issues." ⊗

Jason DaPonte is the founder of consultancy The Swarm and the former head of BBC Mobile

GLOBAL VIEW

|||||||||||||||||||||||||||||||||||||||||||||||||||||||||||||||||||||||||||||||||||||||||||||||||||||||||||||||||||||

45(03): 60/61 I DOI: 10.1177/0306422016670348

The threats from Europe's right-to-be-forgotten legislation are being extended, with newspaper archives being edited and search engines receiving massive fines, says **Jodie Ginsberg**

NEWSPAPER ARCHIVES ARE a matter of record, a window to our past. Deleting links to articles, erasing certain names, puts all that in jeopardy. Yet this is the next step in the European battle for the right to be forgotten.

Under the right-to-be-forgotten ruling, which was first approved by the European Court of Justice in 2014, EU citizens can ask search engines to remove links to information about them.

But in May, a Belgian court went further, it ruled that a newspaper archive should remove the name of a person from a 1994 article. It came after Rossel, the publishers of Belgium's Le Soir newspaper, were sued by a member of the public who had been involved in a traffic accident and who demanded that all reference to the matter be expunged from the paper's archives.

Belgium's Cassation Court (the country's main court of last resort) ruled that the right to be digitally forgotten formed part of the constitutionally guaranteed right to be left in peace in one's private life. The Rossel group argued the ruling opened "the door to the rewriting of history".

To recap on the story so far... the ECJ ruled, in 2014, that individuals who deemed information held about them to be "inadequate, irrelevant or no longer relevant" could request that search engines remove links to such data from searches. It did not matter whether the information was factually accurate, what mattered was that the person involved – and the search engine – considered the information to be no longer relevant about that individual.

The ECJ did include some limited protections for public interest – companies and governments cannot make these requests, only individuals – and the search engines must consider the role played by the person "in public life". But the guidance is minimal. It is up to the search engine to decide whether the information constitutes something of public interest or not.

Initially, the ruling was thought to apply only in the European Union, which meant that anyone searching via, for example, Google.com could easily find deleted links even though they would not show up on European versions, such as Google.co.uk or Google.fr. However, European data authorities argued this was insufficient and, since March this year, Google has also introduced geolocation blocks to searches – meaning that if you use .com to search in France you would not see deleted links. Even then, this has not gone far enough for some.

OVER A HALF A MILLION REQUESTS TO BE FORGOTTEN

Since the ruling, some 5542,868 requests have been made to Google (which accounts for 90% of searches in Europe) relating to 1,656,783 links (as of 31 August 2016). Google no longer gives detailed examples of links it has deleted but The Daily Telegraph reported in 2015 that some of the examples of requests for de-indexing their stories included:

• A story about a British former convent girl jailed in France for running a ring of 600 call girls throughout Europe in 2003.
• An article from 2008 about a former pupil from a leading boarding school who drove his car around the school grounds and crashed after a night out drinking.
• A story which included a section from the "war plan" of Norwegian man Anders Behring Breivik to kill 100 people.
• A story from The Telegraph's property page on a family who gave up London life and moved to Devon.

The French regulator – the Commission Nationale de l'Informatique et des Libertes – fined Google 100,000 euros (US$111,700) in March this year for not delisting more widely. It argued the geolocation block was not sufficient and that the right to privacy should not depend simply on the place from where the search was being conducted. CNIL also argued that extending the right to be forgotten worldwide did not limit freedom of expression because the content itself is not actually deleted – it simply does not appear in search results. There is a flaw in this argument – which is that if the same thinking were applied by all countries, it could easily open the door for authoritarian regimes to whitewash the past everywhere.

"If French law applies globally," wrote Google's general counsel, Kent Walker, in a Le Monde op-ed following the appeal, "how long will it be until other countries – perhaps less open and democratic – start demanding that their laws regulating information likewise have global reach? This order could lead to a global race to the bottom, harming access to information that is perfectly lawful to view in one's own country. For example,

> ## This order could lead to a global race to the bottom, harming access to information that is perfectly legal to view in one's own country

this could prevent French citizens from seeing content that is perfectly legal in France. This is not just a hypothetical concern. We have received demands from governments to remove content globally on various grounds – and we have resisted, even if that has sometimes led to the blocking of our services."

It's certainly a dangerous move. Imagine Russia, China or Iran applying these principles. You can see it is not alarmist to suggest that allowing individuals to decide who sees what worldwide according to vaguely applied principles – and expunge fact from archives – is a major threat to our right to information, our right to privacy and our freedom of expression. ⊗

Jodie Ginsberg is the CEO of Index on Censorship. She tweets @jodieginsberg

IN FOCUS

PICTURED: Russian President Vladimir Putin speaks during a meeting with journalists after a live broadcast in Moscow, Russia, in April 2016

Blot, erase, delete

45(03): 64/68 | DOI: 10.1177/0306422016670349

Author **Hilary Mantel** was mute in childhood but then picked up a pen and let permanent ink flow. Here she writes about the importance of sticking to your words, from battling 1980s newspaper censors in Saudi Arabia to the recent Brexit vote. Illustration by **Molly Crabapple**

I HAVE BEEN TRYING to think back to what it was like when I was seen and not heard: when I was too young to talk: when nothing was transmitted but everything received: when I had the luxury of listening without a reply needed: when I could judge without responsibility: when I simply existed, with no further action required. When you are dumb, the world puts on a show. No one knows what you are thinking, or even if you are thinking, before you are old enough to speak.

It's said I prolonged this situation, to the point of enquiry: "Doesn't she talk, what's wrong with her?" But parents are unreliable witnesses. They make up stories about your infancy to suit what they have decided is your character. Also – though they would never admit this – they mix up siblings, and misreport their early words and deeds. I could flatter myself by claiming I waited to speak till I had something to say. But I guess our first words are stupid ones. And throughout childhood I felt the attraction of sliding back into muteness. If they asked a silly question at school – what I thought was a silly question – I just didn't answer. I kept up this recalcitrance till I was 11. There was a schoolroom crime called "dumb insolence", but I don't think anyone mistook my silence for that offence. I looked so sorry about it, I suppose.

In those days I was groaning under a burden of truth. In my family, as in so many, an active censorship bore on both past and present. There were things you could say in the house, but not out of the house; perhaps there was a third category of things you could say in the garden. It is hard for a child to learn where the boundaries are, and also difficult not to be in the wrong place when adults utter what they regret. Aged eight or so, I seemed to lose my hearing for a year. Anything you said, I asked in a tone of hard incredulity to have repeated: "What?" I must have developed a protective filter, because in time I could hear again. The voice continued to say "What?" but it spoke inside. There were things you knew but must study to unknow, and things that could only be said allegorically. By way of allegory, a child might have a symptom. My brother couldn't catch his breath. No chance of saying the wrong thing, when you couldn't even breathe.

The time comes when you take up the pen. It is mightier than the sword, you hear. In my memoir Giving Up The Ghost, I wrote about the child's toy called the "magic slate", which enabled you to write with a stylus on a sheet of transparent film, and have your writing appear – grey and faint, easily erased by pulling up a tab. I entered into a paradise of free expression, but: "One day the light caught the surface at a certain angle, →

→ and when I held the slate away from me and turned it I saw that the pen left marks in the plastic sheet, like the tracks of writing on water. It would have been possible, with some labour and diligence, to discover the words even after they had been erased. After that I left aside the magic slate…"

At my primary school we wrote with nib pens. Ink was poured into wells which were silted, muddy at the bottom; only the top, to the depth of a fingertip, remained liquid, and if you plunged your pen further in, the nib emerged fuzzy and clogged by the accretions of the generations: the shaving of cedar pencils formed the grit at the bottom of the sump, together with hair torn from the exasperated head, dust motes that had floated in the sunlight before the Great War, compacted paper balls soaked by our grandparents some idle afternoon. Maybe this was why, when I began to write, I wrote like an Edwardian. Some children – some girls – had blotting paper and applied it every three or four words, so that their lines appeared deliberately antiqued, ready-faded, half-expunged. Their process drove me into a frenzy of irritation and dislike: the slow, painful scratch of metal as it snagged rough paper: the goggle-eyed stare at the result, as if the

Ink is a generative fluid. If you don't mean your words to breed consequences, don't write at all

writer had insulted herself: the slow reaching for the pink sheet, the emphatic, vengeful pressure on the page.

I never trusted the blotters. Now they remind me of those people who jump up and wash straight after sex. Ink is a generative fluid. If you don't mean your words to breed consequences, don't write at all; the only tip you can give to a prospective writer is "Try to mean what you say". We feel protected

when we write on a screen, but (as with the magic slate) we can be fooled. Erasure seems simple – blink and it's gone, overwrite the line. But nothing ever really goes away. The internet keeps regurgitating you. You can't bury or burn your traces. They won't be nibbled by rats, who used to love vellum, or munched by tropical ants, or consumed in the small fires that afflicted archives every few years, leaving scorched and partial truths for historians to frown over. You could get nostalgic about holes in the ground, graves for data: about the old days when they buried bad news. It seems you can't hide, repent or change your mind. As soon as you sit before the screen you start haunting yourself.

There was a time, early in my high-school life, when crossing-out was forbidden. No tearing out of pages either. You must show your workings. The painful steps towards error must be clear to all. I think it was a rule made so that our exercise books wouldn't fall apart, but at the time it seemed like a particularly peevish form of persecution and control. When my enemies raided my desk, they attacked my exercise books, but it was the blank sheets they tore out; my enemies were not very bright. At some stage I must have made a commitment to commitment, and to stand by my mistakes, because I noticed that only bubbleheads used washable, bright blue ink, and took to Permanent Black. Accidents will happen, of course. Probably people now won't have breathed it in or seen it: the bitter, metallic, ineradicable spill.

In the early 1980s I went to live in Saudi Arabia, which was then the Empire of Deletion, the world capital of crossing-out. Pre-internet, there was only print to be censored, though certain public sculptures had been removed. There was a street informally known as Thumb Street, though the thumb had been taken down long before we came; it was in case people had the idea of worshipping it, I suppose, for it was irreligious to represent the human form. In those days if you bought an imported newspaper or magazine, the censors had worked through it carefully. They crayoned black drapery across the welling breasts of starlets. They hampered the muscled legs of women athletes by giving them skirts, rudely triangular and sloping at the hem, their brio and haste and hatred and lust all skidding across the picture in big black lines from a permanent marker.

The effort was touching: the meticulous thoroughness. The authorities could have banned the newspaper. But that would attract comment. Besides, an army of highly trained human erasers must have work. I imagined grey hangars on the desert's fringe, where the contaminated material was carried in and out by men in protective suits, moving silently across the roads of the kingdom in unmarked vans. Probably it wasn't like that; but there was no way of finding out how it was. Some of the erasers were charged with reading the back of food packets for recipes, and eradicating the word "pork" wherever it occurred, so removing from the world the very idea of pig. Keep the dietary laws, by all means, but what is forbidden goes tritt-trot through your dreams; pigs came to them by night, I think, pink or piebald, hairy or smooth, huffing in their ears and rolling in their duvets. Yet the effort of deletion persisted. The existence of women was tackled by placing them under black curtains. The existence of Israel was tackled by simply leaving it off the maps.

This army of erasers came back to my mind at the time of the EU referendum, when the urban legend spread that votes for "Leave" would be rubbed out by an army of secret service personnel, and Brexiteers began to take their own pens into the polling booth. How we laughed! But then as soon as the result was in, millions signed a petition to rub it out and do it again. The bien-pensant suggested the result was not binding, but advisory – an opinion they would hardly have offered had the vote gone the other way. For a long time people have suspected

that voting was futile; that politicians did not mean their promises even at the time they made them; that even though they were printed, recorded, filmed, painted on vans and driven about the streets, they could be blinked away, vanished at will. Sometimes

I went to live in Saudi Arabia, which was then the Empire of Deletion, the capital of crossing-out

people speak allegorically, through folk-panics: we make our mark, but they just rub us out. I thought it was odd, when the MP Jo Cox was murdered in the street, that campaigning in the referendum was suspended. She was a politician – and so they stopped politics? If a poet died, would you say, →

→ "Out of respect, ease off the verse?" If a historian died, would you try to stop events? A better tribute to her would have been to continue the campaign, interposing a day in which all parties spoke the truth. But the world is not ready for that kind of memorial. It might violate some untested physical law, so we end in mass-drownings or a ball of fire.

A better tribute to Cox, would have been to continue the campaign, interposing a day in which all parties spoke the truth

It has always been axiomatic that when the dying speak, they cannot lie. I knew a man whose mother told him, as she lay dying, who his real father was: like a woman in a Victorian melodrama. She might as well have climbed out of bed and kicked his feet from under him. The truth was far too late to do him any good, and just in time to plunge him into misery and confusion and the complex grief of a double loss. Some truths have a sell-by date. Some should not be uttered even by the dying. Some cannot be uttered. When a victim of Henry VIII faced the headsman, the standard scaffold speech praised the king: his justice, his mercy. You didn't mean this, but you had to think about the people left behind: some flattery might help them. Oppressors don't just want to do their deed, they want to take a bow: they want their victims to sing their praises. This doesn't change, and it seems there are no new thoughts, no new struggles with censorship and self-censorship, only the old struggles repeating: half-animated corpses of forbidden childhood thoughts crawling out of the psychic trenches we have dug for them, and recurring denials by the great of the truths written on the bodies of the small.

I have 97 notebooks in a wooden box. I do not count them as suppressed volumes. I work on the principle that there is no failed work, only work pending: that there is nothing I won't say, only what I haven't said yet. In my novel in progress I have written, "If you cannot speak truth at a beheading, when can you speak it?" A notebook written eight years ago says, "I am searching for a place where the truth can be uttered: a place, I mean, that is not an execution ground." ⊗

Hilary Mantel is the two-time winner of the Man Booker Prize for her bestselling novels Wolf Hall *and* Bring Up the Bodies. *The Royal Shakespeare Company and the BBC have adapted both works for the stage and screen, respectively. She has written 14 books, including the short-story compilation* The Assassination of Margaret Thatcher *and a memoir,* Giving up the Ghost. *She is currently at work on the third installment of her Thomas Cromwell Trilogy*

Murder in Moscow: Anna's legacy

45(03): 69/74 I DOI: 10.1177/0306422016670350

Andrey Arkhangelsky explores Russian journalism today, 10 years after investigative reporter **Anna Politkovskaya** was killed, and argues that the press still struggles to bring readers the full picture

ON 7 OCTOBER 2006, journalist Anna Politkovskaya was murdered in Moscow. Ten years on, the battle to publish investigative journalism in Russia is still being lost.

When Polikovskaya died, there was speculation of government involvement, an international outcry and various posthumous awards for her investigative work. Yet in Russia there was no scandal, no mass protests. She was mostly deemed a "crazy loner", one of a very rare breed of reporters who believed in press independence.

A decade later, we have a better understanding of Politkovskaya's significance for Russian journalism. Like many of her generation, she was a product of the perestroika years of 1985-91, and remained faithful to its ideals in the years that followed, when a majority of her colleagues "tired of freedom". In the 25 years after perestroika, neither freedom of speech nor other political freedoms have been much prized by the majority of citizens of this new Russia.

In the 2000s, Politkovskaya's stance was regarded as extreme. Who was there to fight against anyway? For what? The years of plenty were at their peak. Sooner or later economics would win and everything would sort itself out. Even liberals believed that.

It is important to understand the tradition to which Anna belonged. For her, being a journalist meant serving society, a tradition of self-sacrifice dating back to the 19th-century Russian intelligentsia. In the Soviet period this tradition was inherited by dissidents. In Russia, the line between journalism and social activism remains blurred, and not because Russian journalists are unprofessional, but because independence of the press has remained the ideal of rare characters such as Politkovskaya. There is no long-standing tradition of media independence. Each generation of journalists instinctively chooses between fusing completely with the state, which means producing propaganda and giving loyal support, or remaining steadfastly professional and inwardly dissident. Working as a journalist in Russia is not so much pursuing a profession as living an ethical, existential choice.

POLITKOVSKAYA WORKED AS an investigative journalist for Novaya Gazeta. Novaya Gazeta, which was founded in 1994, is probably the only publication that has consistently practised investigative journalism from the outset. Since 2000, more journalists and staff from Novaya Gazeta have been murdered than from any other publication: Yury Schekochikhin, Igor Domnikov, Anna →

Politkovskaya, Anastasia Baburova, Stanislav Markelov, Natalia Estemirova and others. The Russian-language New Times magazine, edited by Yevgenia Albats, also remains true to the investigative genre, as did, until recently, the media group RBC. From 2014 RBC published a succession of high-profile investigations into the activities of major companies, top-ranking Kremlin officials and their relatives. But on 13 May 2016 the group's editor Yelizaveta Osetinskaya and others were fired after reports of Kremlin pressure on the group's holding company Onexim and RBC's management.

Investigative journalism had already disappeared from other publications. It is expensive as well as dangerous. Investigation is labour-intensive, it calls for a large team and takes a lot of time. The speed of modern media obliges editors to churn out instant

VIOLATIONS AGAINST THE PRESS IN RUSSIA

21 July 2016: Andrey Nazarenko, a cameraman from All-Russia State Television and Radio Broadcasting Company (VGTRK), was found shot dead in his Moscow apartment.

14 July 2016: The house of Elena Suslova, deputy editor of independent newspaper Otkrytaya Gazeta, was fire-bombed, which she believed to be in connection with her work. She has covered allegations of corruption in regional elections and abuse of power by local officials.

11 May 2016: Deputy editor-in-chief of local newspaper Minuta Istiny, Oleg Kunitsyn, was shot twice by an unknown attacker, one bullet hitting him in the shoulder. The editor believes the attack may have been connected to reports published by the newspaper on the alleged corruption of Vologda's mayor, Evgeni Shulepov.

2 December 2015: Two members of a film crew from Russia-24 television channel were severely physically assaulted by the mayor of the city Ulan-Ude, Alexander Golkov, and his deputies during an interview. Journalist Artem Kol and cameraman Vladimir Bragin were attacked after they questioned the official about a New Year's bonus of 320,000 rubles (US$4,935) he received from the local budget.

28 August 2015: The flat of blogger and poet Aleksandr Byvshev was raided by the central department for counter-extremism for the Russian ministry for internal affairs. Byvshev, whose blog published a number of his verses dedicated to the Ukrainian democratic changes, had USB sticks, a PC and a laptop seized.

21 August 2015: A team of journalists working for Stavropolie TV were attacked by guards of the mineral extraction site in Kochubeevski district of Stavropol Krai while they were shooting the illegal excavation of minerals. The guards threw stones at the cameraman and the team's car, and stole their keys.

31 July 2014: Timur Kuashev, a correspondent for Dosh magazine, went missing from his home. His body was found the following day in a forest in the suburb of Nalchik. Kuashev, whose work includes the investigation of the abuses by the security forces in anti-terrorism operations, had been receiving threats for years and published an open letter in April 2013 expressing concern for his life.

Josie Timms and MMF correspondents
Source: Mappingmediafreedom.org

copy. That, however, is not the main reason why there are so few investigations in the Russian media. And the disbanding of the top team at RBC after it launched a series of investigations into senior state officials sent a signal to other media.

Most resonant investigations of recent years though have not been the work of journalists, but of politicians of one kind or another. The flagship of investigative journalism in Russia remains the Anti-Corruption Foundation (FBK), a non-profit foundation created in 2011 by the opposition activist Alexey Navalny. It conducts the most high-profile investigations of corrupt senior officials, and they are carried out by a highly professional investigative team of 20 to 30 lawyers, specialists and volunteers.

Similarly, the first person to write in 2014 about the secret funerals of Russian paratroopers when the military conflict in the Donbass region was escalating was Lev Shlosberg. Although Shlosberg publishes Pskovskaya Gazeta, he is primarily a politician.

We can also classify as journalistic investigative reporting, the 2008 document, Putin: The Results: An Independent Expert Report written by opposition politicians Boris Nemtsov and Vladimir Milov. The report described President Putin's abuse of power and widespread corruption in government.

The paradox is that, in Russia today, no amount of scandalous revelations of corruption at the highest level sways public opinion. For most people, the findings remain unknown, because 80% of the population get their news only from television.

TV aside, the most popular form of journalism in Russia today is the topical opinion column. Until the mass protests against Putin in 2012, it was thought this, too, was defunct and that nobody was interested in the personal opinions of a journalist. Yet it was the columnists who, that year, restored journalism's intellectual respectability by starting serious and engaging conversations about freedom and human rights. Many of them

have since become important public figures.

In Russia, the side dish has become the main dish. For example, Slon.ru, a business, economics and politics website founded in 2009, consists entirely of opinion pieces,

ABOVE: A man lays flowers near the picture of murdered journalist Anna Politkovskaya, during a rally in Moscow in 2009

Independence of the press has remained the ideal of so-called "crazy loners" like Politkovskaya

which sometimes turn into mini-investigations, particularly when the author is Oleg Kashin.

Kashin is a good example of this new trend of favouring individual writers over newspapers – a trend which has grown largely thanks to social networks, especially Facebook and Twitter. Kashin showed the power of self-publishing by building the →

III

INTO THE FUTURE, AND INTO THE PAST

Below is an extract from an interview with Anna Politkovskaya, published in Index on Censorship in 2005. We republish this for the 10th anniversary of her murder

Vladimir Putin has said that Russia will not allow foreigners to finance our civil society, but now we have no domestic investors to do it, which is a tragedy. If we continue like this, 100 years years from now there will be no civil society in Russia.

Tragically, our most active democrats are on the Left. I cannot bring myself to vote Communist because the distance between their progressive and repressive instincts is too short, but Putin's regime is a great recruiting ground for the Left, particularly among the young.

The media will share the fate of the rest of the country. My newspaper, Novaya Gazeta, will do all it can to stay open, but there are no grounds for optimism. Two years ago, we had points of contact with Putin; now there are none. He said, "We will fight our enemies" so it's either him or us. "Us" meaning the "voice of protest".

The Union of Writers consists of people who show they are writers by chumming up to the Kremlin. As an organisation that receives perks from the government it is an absolute non-starter, a relic of the USSR. If Russia develops democratically, there will be no Writers' Union in the future, just a professional trade union for writers. Traditionally, we have needed film directors, artists and writers to tell people what a great country they live in. But that has nothing to do with writing or intellectual endeavour, or with the effort to depict life as it is.

I love my country but I don't want it to have a "Special Way". I want it to be just like other countries where there is democracy and the police protect people from criminals instead of oppressing them. I want us to be like everyone else. People who talk about a "Special Way" usually want to oppress somebody.

I hope there will be no registration system in the future (the system under which the USSR controlled its citizens by registering them in a particular place). In a country the size of Russia you can't hope to keep track of everyone. Registration is just a system for extorting bribes and without it a person becomes a nobody: no education, no medical help, no pension. It has brought us so much suffering that if we develop into a democracy I cannot imagine it surviving.

The full article can be found in the Index archive:
ioc.sagepub.com

→ audience of his own website via social networks. Journalist and writer Arkady Babchenko, who carried out a one-man investigation into the shootings on Kiev's Maidan Square in 2014, has the same approach.

This method is one way to survive, as journalists increasingly find it impossible to maintain an independent point of view while working for state owned, or even privately owned, media. What other ways are there? Besides the already well-established route of emigration from Russia to Ukraine, a route taken by Yevgeny Kiselyov, Savik Shuster, Matvey Gannpolsky, Ivan Yakovina and the recently murdered Pavel Sheremet, there are more exotic choices. The Medusa media portal, an independent Russian language sociopolitical network publication, is registered in Latvia. Galina Timchenko founded it in 2014, together with a group of former staff members, after she was sacked as editor-in-chief of Lenta.ru, the Moscow-based online newspaper.

Two processes are taking place in Russia almost simultaneously: restriction of free speech, and technological progress in the media sphere. This creates a strong sense of absurdity. In 2008-12, during the presidency of Dmitry Medvedev, there was a major breakthrough in new media technology, which coincided with the growth of the middle class. New standards were set, as a demand rose for stories about politics, human rights, migrants and problems in society. This was seen not only by business publications like the business daily Vedomosti, the liberal business broadsheet Kommersant, and the Russian edition of Forbes magazine, but also by cultural and listings magazines such as Afisha, which is now published mainly online and Bolshoy Gorod, which closed down in 2013.

This complication of this scene culminated with the appearance of a new kind of publication, Openspace.ru, a news site for Russia's creative vanguard, founded in 2008 by Maria Stepanova and Gleb Morev. Since 2013 the two partners have also been running the cultural magazine and news site Colta.ru. The internet seems to have given journalists more freedom and even made it possible to raise funds independently. A paid subscription scheme was successfully introduced for the first time by the Slon.ru, who started their project by crowdfunding.

Before the 2012 protests, the Kremlin did not see internet publications as a threat: its total control of television ensured the loyalty of 70-80% of the electorate. When Medvedev came to power this balance even shifted slightly in favour of channels with smaller audiences. The Dozhd channel, dubbed "Television for intelligent people", targeted the middle class and was founded in 2010. Part of Medvedev's liberalisation project also included an independent and non-commercial

public television channel (OTR), which he set into motion but which only started broadcasting in 2014.

It is significant that the main weapon of the "conservative restoration", after Putin returned for a third term in 2012, was the traditional media of television and radio. There was not only a counter attack by those with anti-liberal values but also by the traditional media. Technology on its own proved inadequate for resisting the mechanisms of the state: that could be done only by people who had opinions.

IN JULY, AN enlightening conversation was leaked. RBC, now under new management after the previous staff were fired, held a meeting between management and journal-

Before the 2012 protests, the Kremlin did not see internet publications as a threat

ists. One RBC reporter asked where the line should be drawn when reporting. Which topics, in other words, did the publication feel it could no longer cover? He received the answer: "That, unfortunately, nobody knows." It is a response that encapsulates the predicament of the media in Russia which are trying to maintain a degree of freedom. It is a hole journalism has dug for itself.

Publishers and investors used to think that if they played by the rules and avoided open criticism of the Kremlin, no one would touch them. The rules are, however, constantly changing, and they aren't written down anywhere. One can only second guess them. This Kafkaesque situation gives rise to a general sense of nervousness, but also tells us something about freedom of speech: anyone who voluntarily agrees to partial curtailment of their freedom will sooner or later have it taken away completely.

→ While resolving its practical problems by introducing new censorship laws, by emasculating such leading information platforms as Lenta.ru and the Russian-language news agency RIA-Novosti, by blocking such sites as Kasparov.ru and Polit.ru, and removing a number of editors-in-chief, the regime also accomplished a symbolic task. It managed to discredit the very notion of an independent press in the eyes of the general public. The conservative restoration in Russia since 2012 has been a struggle against anything that is "above" the state, specifically, against the idea of universal values and freedom of speech.

Most media have already lost the battle. Journalists have no experience of closing ranks to defend their rights, and most private owners are willing to abandon freedom of speech in order to retain their businesses.

Journalists are forced to make a moral choice, where the line between good and evil is drawn

The disbanding of teams of journalists in 2013-16 was generally explained away as being for commercial reasons: "the unviability of the publication". Only in two cases did the Kremlin not get away with this ploy. The Dozhd television channel and the radio station Echo of Moscow put up a spirited all-round defence involving the editors, the staff, and the viewers or listeners. Amazingly enough, in both cases, the regime was unable to get them to abandon their critical stance.

The main target of government attacks in the future is likely to be the internet, with an attempt to take control of social networks. The recently adopted Yarovoy law increases the burden of responsibility for anyone whose internet postings could be deemed "extremist", and obliges communications operators to keep recordings of all calls and messages, metadata, exchanged between

users for six months. The same applies to internet service providers, who are obliged to keep metadata for three years. The presidential adviser on the internet industry, Herman Klimenko, appears to be considering the option of an autonomous Russian internet, analogous to that of China. "If we close our borders now, I mean virtually, all our sites will benefit," he said in a recent interview with the BBC Russian service.

Under these conditions, journalism in Russia is often simply unable to perform the basic function of journalism, which is to inform the public about what is happening. Independent journalism does what it can, and by the very fact of its existence reminds people that alternative opinions about universal human values are possible. It provides an alternative to propaganda. The only good thing about the profession today is that people working in journalism are forced, much sooner than others, to make a moral choice where the line between good and evil is to be drawn.

Ten years after her murder, the example of Anna Politkovskaya is relevant to all of us. ⊗

Andrey Arkhangelsky is a Russian journalist and columnist. He is culture editor at Ogonyok magazine

*Translated by **Arch Tait***

Writing in riddles

|||||||||||||||||||||||||||||||||||||||||||||||||||||||||||||||||||||||||||||||||||

45(03): 75/77 | DOI: 10.1177/0306422016670351

In the Soviet era, censorship forced authors to resort to metaphors and parables. This allusive language has become so entrenched in Russian literature that it is holding writers back from tackling today's problems, argues Uzbek author **Hamid Ismailov**

ONE OF THE most famous metaphors in Russian literature is the blizzard. Nearly all great Russian writers have, at least once, described these sudden snowstorms, when in the middle of Russia's immense empty spaces, a wayfarer or a carriage loses its way, is taken hostage by "white devil's dance", and ends up in an unintended place and situation.

Russian writers love metaphor. It's easy to see why. During the Soviet era, Leonid Brezhnev's clique found itself failing to change the world, and began to change the words instead – renaming places, recreating history, creating new simulacra, and all to make people believe that they were living in a perfect socialist world. Writers opposing the regime responded by creating a coded literature, full of hints, allusions and metaphors, leaving perceptive readers to find the real meaning between the lines.

Today, even though the break-up of the Soviet Union and the short period of reigning liberalism in Russia has led to many changes, literature has stayed the same. Editors of literary magazines, publishers, critics and, consequently, the writers themselves have become so accustomed to this type of overly coded literature that it has never gone away.

The "best" of the living Russian novelists, the ones who win awards and literary acclaim, are still obsessed with intellectual jigsaws, enigmatic parables and high-brow exercises. Their way of reflecting the current reality of Russia is expressed through Buddhist philosophy (Victor Pelevin's Omon Ra or Chapayev and Void), historical parallels with medieval Russia (Vladimir Sorokin's Day of the Oprichnik, Eugene Vodolazkin's Laurus) or utopian or dystopian narratives (Mikhail Shishkin's Letter Book or Dmitry Bykov's Jewhad).

This leaves straightforward prose to journalists, from the late Anna Politkovskaya [see page 69] to Arkady Babchenko, a soldier-turned-war correspondent who wrote a book about war in Chechnya. Or to non-fiction writers, such as the winner of the latest Nobel prize for literature, Svetlana Alexievich from Belarus.

Though political art exists, it tends to come in other forms, from pop-punk group Pussy Riot and their protest performance in an Orthodox cathedral, to artist Pyotr Pavlensky, who sewed his mouth shut and nailed himself to the Red Square. (In June, Pavlensky was charged with vandalism and fined for setting fire to the door of Russia's security service headquarters in protest.)

Switching to writing manifestos, social pamphlets or "realist" literature isn't the answer. But in Russia and many post-Soviet countries, the oblique, jigsaw-like canon of fiction writing has gained undue prominence at the expense of other, more direct styles →

The "best" of the living Russian novelists are still obsessed with intellectual jigsaws, enigmatic parables and high-brow exercises

→ of writing. This has become a new form of restriction. It is not state-imposed censorship, nor self-censorship, but a sort of control that comes from your literary peers, critics, publishers and some readers – one that is dictated by the expectations of the whole industry.

As we approach the 100th anniversary of the 1917 revolution, I find the old Russian classics are more relevant to our times.

ABOVE: Statue of a girl reading in the Moscow Metro

On recently re-reading Notes of a Stranger by Nikolai Leskov, written nearly 150 years ago, I was surprised to find it related to current realities much more than any recent prizewinner. Leskov dares to tackle corruption in society and even in the Orthodox church – an issue that is extremely acute in today's Russia. Modern writers who do the same risk rejection from the establishment.

But does this mean the great Russian literature is becoming a kind of "glass bead game", an elitist priesthood? Should we expect a backlash from younger writers and readers? Russian poetry, for instance, has moved on. The coded "meta-metaphoric" poetry of the late Soviet period has already been replaced by a fresh, more direct new wave.

Take one of the leading literary figures of Russia, Dmitry Bykov, whose project Citizen Poet was extremely topical and very successful. It saw actors reciting Bykov's satirical verses about Russian politics and society. First broadcast online in 2011, via the Dozhd (Rain) channel, it later moved to Echo of Moscow radio station. Bykov's journalism is similarly direct in style. Yet his novels remain rather enigmatic and symbolic.

For the rest of Russian literature to move forward, it needs to expand beyond Moscow and St Petersburg. It needs an influx of "other" voices, from the provinces – especially from the ethnically diverse ones. It could benefit from the same expansion as, say, postcolonial Britain, where literature was enriched by the likes of VS Naipaul, Derek Walcott, Salman Rushdie, Chinua Achebe and Ngũgĩ wa Thiong'o.

This is happening in Russian literature, but slowly. Different perspectives are coming from Alisa Ganieva from Dagestan, Guzel Yakhina from Tatarstan, Suhbat Aflatuni from Uzbekistan, and Russian writers with experience of living on the fringes of Russia, such as Alexey Slapovsky, Roman Senchin and Alexander Terekhov. Contemporary Russia's great narrative is the search for its identity, a new place in the world after the collapse of the Soviet Union, and those writers are better placed to address that.

Much of my criticism of modern Russian literature is true of the Uzbek contemporary literature as well. Authors considered the "best" of modern Uzbek writers by the country's literary critics are those who are writing pseudo-Sufi parables. These are oblique tales, the sort that use a fable about a goldfish in a tank in order to criticise the social passivity of people.

Those who dare to write about the horrid conditions of life in modern-day Uzbekistan, about the millions who are migrating to Russia and other places to make a living, about the thousands upon thousands being arrested and tortured for their beliefs, about the prostitute girls and destitute boys leaving

schools uneducated: they end up either in prison or in a mental institution. And this is not a metaphor, but the grim reality, which people like Mamadali Makhmudov, Yusuf Juma, Muhammad Bekjan, Dilmurad Sayid, Diloram Iskhakova, Mutabar Tadjibayeva, Salomat Vafo and many others have faced.

When I was young, there was a game that children used to play. You would walk from a distance of 10 steps away towards a small

For Russian literature to move forward, it needs an influx of voices from the provinces, and from other ethnicities

box of matches and try to flick it with a finger, but deliberately miss it, nine times in a row. The 10th time you would ask another person to try to flick the box, but against all odds he or she would usually miss it too. This innocent game comes to my mind as I think about the future of Uzbek literature. As the experience of Russia demonstrates, even when given the liberty to write, many people carry on with their myths and parables.

I can't resist a parable myself. This one is about an old folk hero, Hodja Nasreddin, who was sometimes simple, sometimes wise.

"Hodja, last night I was passing by your house and I heard a lot of commotion. What was that all racket?"

"Nothing serious. My wife threw my coat down the stairs."

"Hodja, how could a coat falling down the stairs make that much noise?"

"At the time, I happened to be in it!"

Unless you fill the empty coat of metaphors and parables with something substantial, it seems that there's no noise … ⊗

Hamid Ismailov is the BBC World Service's Central Asia editor. His latest novel is The Underground (Restless Books, 2015)

CREDIT: Juan Mabromata / AFP /Getty Images

Owners of our own words

45(03): 78/81 | DOI:10.1177/0306422016670352

When Argentinian newspaper Tiempo Argentino lost funding after a change in government, the staff decided to go it alone as a co-operative – but it turned nasty when their offices were violently attacked. **Irene Caselli** reports from Buenos Aires

IT WAS IN the early hours of the morning when a group of men stormed the offices of Tiempo Argentino newspaper in Buenos Aires' upmarket Palermo neighbourhood on 4 July. The newly formed collective that ran the publication said men forcibly removed journalists, smashed a wall, cut the internet and phone lines, and destroyed equipment, furniture, archives and documents. Their sister radio station Radio América also had much of its equipment ruined.

"They didn't steal anything. They were clearly here to break things, to make us stop producing the paper and going on air," Javier Borelli, president of the co-operative, told Index after the attack.

LEFT: A worker checks the damages at the office at Tiempo Argentino newspaper in Buenos Aires on 4 July 2016

RIGHT: A portrait of murdered Argentinian journalist Rodolfo Walsh was smashed in the July raid. Index on Censorship published Walsh's open letter to the military junta in 1977

→ By this point staff had already been through months of upheaval. Under the previous president, Cristina Fernández de Kirchner, they were establishment darlings. Adopting a pro-government position had won the publication major state advertising deals. But when a new president, Marci Macri, was elected in December 2015, this funding dried up. Their employer stopped paying their salaries, and the new owner, who was believed to be businessman Mariano Martínez Rojas, had not paid any bills.

Worse still, Martínez Rojas was seen accompanying the heavies into the building on that July morning. Photographs showed him leaving the destroyed building with a police guard. Journalists at the co-operative had long been suspicious that the sale was a

This attack is unprecedented since Argentina's return to democracy. It's one of the worst attacks on freedom of expression

set-up by the previous owners to wash their hands of the business.

"This attack is unprecedented since Argentina's return to democracy," Gabriel Michi, a member of the Argentinian Journalism Forum (Fopea) and reporter for Radio América, told Index, referring to the end of the military dictatorship in 1983. "It's one of the worst attacks against freedom of expression."

The new government also condemned the attack, releasing a statement on the same day, which said workers were "victims of the irresponsible actions of a group of businessmen". But the co-operative was worried by remarks made by President Macri, who said that "any type of misappropriation is bad" when referring to the co-operative's use of the office.

After Macri took office, Grupo 23, which owned several publications, including Tiempo Argentino, a TV channel and three radio stations, saw its close relationship with the government end abruptly. The following month its sale was announced.

During the period between 2009 and 2015, Grupo 23 received more than 800 million Argentinian pesos (US$53 million) from the previous government, more than any other media group in the country, according to an investigation by La Nación newspaper. The connection to former President Fernández was also apparent in the paper's editorial position, which was supportive of the government's socially oriented policies and vocal against the opposition: so much so critics accused it of publishing propaganda.

In March 2016, Tiempo Argentino relaunched itself, inspired by another Argentinian media co-operative, lavaca, and many recovered factories that were taken over by workers following Argentina's financial crash in 2001. "Owners of our own words" was the strapline. The first self-managed edition appeared on 24 March 2016 and, on the same day, sold 35,000 copies at a march that marked the 40th anniversary of Argentina's military coup. It was a significant improvement compared to the 7,000 copies sold daily in the last months of 2015, according to representatives of the co-operative, which has called itself Por Más Tiempo (which translates as For More Tiempo, or, literally, For More Time, playing on the idea that they are here to stay).

"It was the first money we had seen since December 2015. We split it among all the workers and left some aside to finance →

the following edition," Borelli told Index.

The paper now functions as an online daily and appears in print on Sundays. Directors, editors and reporters (120 in total), and also assistants and cleaners, earn the same amount per hour. This has meant a pay cut for editors and directors, but others earn the same or more than before. Since March, the paper has already published several scoops and set the news agenda. For example, it was the first paper to delve deeper into information about Macri's undeclared offshore companies, a story initially revealed by the Panama papers' leak and denied by the president himself. "We believe there are other ways of doing journalism," said Borelli. "It's harder because there is less money around, but self-management makes us independent from the economic and political powers."

In the immediate aftermath of the attack on Tiempo's newspaper offices, a Buenos Aires prosecutor indicted Martínez Rojas and the other men for usurping and damaging the newsroom. Journalists were told they could continue to work in the building and the state has provided them with security. The ministry of labour had already given custody of the building to the co-operative back in March, while judicial proceedings were started against the owners for missed rent payments.

Yet Borelli remains concerned, and the co-operative's lawyer has called for an investigation into the police's role on the night of the raid. "Macri himself never condemned the attack," said Borelli. "Today Tiempo Argentino is one of the few media that is opposed to his administration. He's sending us a message."

In an email exchange with Index, Hernán Lombardi, the minister in charge of public media, did not refer to Macri's comments, but he did condemn the incidents. "An attack against any media is an attack against a sacred public good: freedom of press and the circulation of ideas," he said. "We can't forget that during the previous government there were businessmen that filled their pockets. Those who worked at the newspaper were the first ones to be harmed by the mismanagement of the owners and of the previous government, who used the money of all Argentines to create media that clearly could not sustain themselves."

According to Martín Becerra, an independent media analyst at Argentina's National Scientific and Technical Research

Directors, editors, reporters, assistants and cleaners all earn the same amount per hour

Council, the government has not done enough to protect Tiempo Argentino and its sister radio station Radio América. "The attack compromises freedom of expression of media with which the current administration has shown an attitude of superiority and has refused to deal with," Becerra told Index.

Becerra also said that the current media landscape is challenging in terms of the idea of plurality.

Under the last government, the opposition found space to express their voice in private media such as the Clarín group and La Nación newspaper, which were openly against the previous administrations. But that is not the case now.

"As I see it now, the media landscape is very unbalanced. There are voices with much presence, power and audience that are generally very friendly towards Macri, and there is no counterbalance in terms of criticism of the current administration, which is necessary in a democracy," said Becerra. ⊗

Irene Caselli is a freelance journalist based in Argentina. She has worked in South America for the past decade for the BBC and the Washington Post, among others

CREDIT: Mike Hutchings/Reuters

Sackings, South Africa and silence

45(03): 82/85 I DOI: 10.1177/0306422016670353

Is public broadcasting doomed to failure in southern Africa? **Natasha Joseph** looks at the power of government to influence television news

VUYO MVOKO KNOWS more about doing his job at gunpoint than most journalists would like to. The seasoned South African broadcaster and a crew were preparing to do a live broadcast from outside a Johannesburg hospital in March 2015 when two armed men robbed them. The entire incident was captured on live television.

Little more than a year later, Mvoko found himself in the crosshairs again. This time the weapon in question was the censorship wielded by his own employer, the South African Broadcasting Corporation.

Mvoko became one of the so-called SABC 8. Seven were journalists, who were summarily sacked by the country's massive public broadcaster after they'd stood up against repeated instances of censorship. Mvoko, who was a freelancer, had his contract terminated. All but Mvoko (at the time of publication) were reinstated after court action.

Mvoko wrote an exposé for the Independent Group of newspapers about his "hell" at the broadcaster, outlining several instances in which the now former head of news Jimi Matthews and the SABC's controversial chief operating officer Hlaudi Motsoeneng had blocked him from asking "tough" questions of senior African National Congress leaders. The broadcaster is accused by many of being the personal mouthpiece of the governing party, an allegation echoed by Matthews after his own very public resignation.

How has the influential public broadcaster reached this point? Post-apartheid South Africa has been considered something of a lodestar for media freedom in the 22 years since it became a democracy. Public broadcasting has been a crucial quiver in the country's bow.

Public broadcasting is generally defined as having a mission of public service to the whole community, and usually receives funds, but operates independently, from governments. It is particularly important in sub-Saharan Africa which doesn't enjoy the sort of internet access which would allow a greater choice of media. People in poorer countries such as Zimbabwe and Swaziland – and even in economically steadier South Africa – can't afford high data costs. They also don't have the sort of continuous access to electricity that's needed for keeping phones and other mobile devices going. Wi-Fi is far from ubiquitous. Many rely on public broadcasters such as SABC as a rare news source. SABC's biggest radio station, Ukhozi FM, has an audience of 6.38 million, while national TV channel SABC1 has viewing figures of 29.5 million.

All of this means the SABC and its regional counterparts ought to be powerful

forces for democracy, debate and independent news coverage. William Bird, the director of Media Monitoring Africa, told Index: "At its best the SABC offers programmes and information in all our [11] official languages. At best it offers unique and niche programming and also offers the greatest diversity of views and programmes. At best it offers something for everyone, so that people feel their lives and stories are reflected in some form. At best it offers the best quality news and training ground for new and emerging journalists and ideas."

But the SABC is far from at its best today. This is partly related to its torrid history.

Like its equivalent to the north, the Zimbabwean Broadcasting Corporation, SABC began life as a political tool for white minority rulers. The SABC was founded in 1936, just over a decade before the advent of for-

The SABC has never been a paragon of a great anything. It has been a work in progress

mal apartheid. Those who expected it would simply shrug off those shackles at the advent of democracy have been proved repeatedly wrong. As Mvoko wrote, in the open letter that caused so much trouble for him: "The SABC has never been a paragon of a great anything. It has been a work in progress, with degrees of success as generations of well-meaning South Africans tackled the extraordinarily complex task of undoing decades of apartheid misuse of this national asset."

The coverage of the 1976 Soweto riots was one of those successes. At the very height of apartheid, SABC reported on riots which saw tens of thousands of black students take to the streets to oppose the mandatory teaching of Afrikaans in schools. Although the coverage was limited, it was one of the seminal moments in South Africa's history →

OPPOSITE: Demonstrators rally outside the offices of SABC in Johannesburg in July. They were protesting against alleged bias and self-censorship in news coverage ahead of key municipal elections

→ and the pictures on TV of the riots was one of the tipping points which eventually ended the apartheid regime.

Almost exactly 40 years on, some accuse the SABC of not reporting on important demonstrations. In June this year there were protests in South Africa's capital city Tshwane (Pretoria) where scores of people took to its streets to protest the ruling ANC's choice of mayoral candidate ahead of the local government elections in August. Buses were burned, roads were barricaded with tyres and rubble, and shops owned by foreigners from elsewhere in Africa were looted. Five deaths were reported. But if, like most people, you relied almost entirely on SABC for your news you would not have been aware it was happening.

Days before Tshwane went up in flames,

Days before Tshwane went up in flames the broadcaster issued an editorial directive banning protest footage and coverage

the broadcaster issued an editorial directive banning protest footage and coverage from its television stations, radio shows and websites. Why? Because the broadcaster ruled, the destruction of public property – which is common during protests in South Africa – is "destructive and regressive". It later added that protesters who destroy clinics, buses, schools and other public infrastructure shouldn't be given any attention or encouragement by journalists.

The move drew massive criticism. Other media groups, civil society organisations, ordinary South Africans and, eventually, the ANC, slammed it as censorship. The directive was then overturned by the Independent Communications Authority of South Africa, which regulates the broadcasting sector. Chief operations officer Motsoeneng initially

vowed to ignore the regulator and challenge its ruling in court, but later announced that the ban on protest footage would be lifted.

Bird told Index that while the protest footage ban had galvanised civil society, a creeping censorship had been apparent at the broadcaster for some time.

"Previously as much as some may have tried and succeeded in certain cases to censor, the place is so large and diverse and has so many systems that it was virtually impossible," Bird said. "What makes this current trend so worrying is that the various systems are being deliberately broken down. [This is] damaging the institution, encouraging fear and greater self-censorship and also doing long term damage."

He also blamed increasingly poor ministerial choices and laws for a "gradual undermining of independence and a tendency towards facilitated chaos".

"All of this provides fertile ground for self-censorship," he added.

It also turns any public broadcaster's role on its head. After all, how can the SABC live up to its own promise to provide South Africans with the information and news reporting they need to participate in building democracy if it's selective in what it shows or doesn't?

Excerpts from an affidavit that Mvoko filed before South Africa's Labour Court to appeal his dismissal bear this out. Independent media commentator, columnist and author Eusebius McKaiser shared parts of the affidavit in a Facebook status towards the end of July. According to Mvoko, he was censured by the acting political editor for making a comment considered supportive of the opposition Democratic Alliance. Motsoeneng himself was allegedly upset and the acting political editor said Motsoeneng scrutinised "each and every word". The implication, McKaiser pointed out, was obvious: "A chilling effect to dissuade journalists from saying anything on air that is even vaguely perceived to be critical of the ANC."

Sekoetlane Phamodi, the national co-ordinator of the civil society group Save Our SABC Coalition, blamed "executive creep" for many of the SABC's current failings. He also cautioned against assuming that the broadcaster's problems have come out of nowhere. Phamodi said that, as in Zimbabwe and Swaziland, there has been a "slow and concerted creep" towards censorship. For example, much has been made of Motsoeneng's call for "positive news" to outweigh anything perceived as negative reporting. But as Phamodi pointed out, an aversion to bad news (particularly anything that would paint the ANC government in a poor light) dates back to the early 2000s under a previous chief executive, Snuki Zikalala. Zikalala also spearheaded the blacklisting of commentators who were perceived to be against the then president Thabo Mbeki. History, as is so often the case, is repeating itself.

Phamodi and his colleagues are especially concerned by the level of executive control the communications minister Faith Muthambi wields over the SABC. Muthambi completely ignored a report by the Office of the Public Protector that found Motsoeneng had lied about his qualifications and was guilty of financial mismanagement. The report suggested that Motsoeneng should not hold a leadership role at the SABC. Muthambi responded by making the appointment permanent.

In July, the ANC finally publicly criticised Motsoeneng and the broadcaster's policies, after which seven of the SABC journalists were reinstated. Whether this is the start of a sea change at SABC remains to be seen. For now, Motsoeneng is in the driving seat and what could be a powerful force for building democracy is severely hamstrung.

Those who support freedom of speech will be hoping SABC is back to its best very soon. ⊗

Natasha Joseph is an Index on Censorship contributing editor, based in Cape Town

SABC TIMELINE

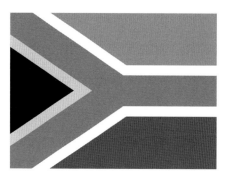

1936: SABC formed (radio only)

1948: Start of formal apartheid

1976: TV comes to South Africa

1994: South Africa becomes a democracy

1996: A major reorganisation sees the broadcaster move to represent black African languages more comprehensively

2000-2005: The SABC is increasingly criticised as a political mouthpiece; it is viewed as being heavily biased towards the governing ANC and found to have blacklisted commentators viewed as being against President Thabo Mbeki.

It is also draws criticism for an interview with Zimbabwe's President Robert Mugabe which avoids tough questions.

2012: Just before the ANC's elective conference, Hlaudi Motsoeneng becomes acting chief operations officer. He is widely viewed as a supporter of President Jacob Zuma, who wins a second term at the conference.

Under Motsoeneng SABC has been dogged by scandal. He has repeatedly called on the media to offer a more positive take on the country; has allegedly spearheaded the blocking of programmes critical of Zuma and in June 2016 ordered that no footage of anti-government protests be broadcast.

"Journalists must not feel alone"

||||||||||||||||||||||||||||||||||||||||||||||||||||||||||||||||||||||||||||||||||||||||||||||||||||||||||||||||||

45(03): 86/87 I DOI: 10.1177/0306422016670354

Award-winning Turkish journalist **Can Dündar** calls for German journalists to pick up the investigation he was forced to abandon

INVESTIGATIVE JOURNALISM IS at a crossroads. One road leads to a new media order where no one feels there is a need for it. The other makes investigative journalism the only alternative to superficial news reporting.

It has an honourable past. It has defended the common good from powerful groups under many different headlines: from war lies to child abuse, human trafficking to stock market manipulation, political skullduggery to dossiers on corruption. It has overthrown presidents and ended wars.

Investigative journalism has changed the world, prevented injustice and informed humanity. It is driven by people who combine scepticism with bravery and patience.

But it is now tired. The traditional media has lost readers. Investment has declined and investigations require time, budgets and manpower.

Attacks on investigative journalists have increased. Desk journalism and sensational reporting have predominated. And increasing amounts of information have created the illusion of a transparent world.

Information today is being hidden in legal loopholes, behind the phrasing of complex legislation which enables corruption and allows it to be secretly stashed away. Or else hidden in the haystacks of data piled up in front of the public.

The biggest difficulty, and most important responsibility, of investigative journalism is to distill the useful information from this data, sort out the parts which serve the public good, turn this all into knowledge, and present this in an easy way for a public accustomed to infotainment to understand.

Take the example of the Panama papers: we have the biggest data leak in history. We're talking about a data haystack of 12 million pages. To scan through the offshore accounts of thousands of businessmen and politicians, locate the irregularities and expose the network of relationships could take decades.

But we do have one chance: international solidarity.

Ever-widening communication networks not only create opportunities for the cooperation of global capital, but also present the same opportunities for solidarity among journalists.

A good example of this is the International Consortium of Investigative Journalists. The group, which calls itself "the world's best cross-border investigative team", has expanded to include 190 journalists from 65 countries. Under the group's leadership, journalists in different countries have begun deciphering the web of power relationships in their own regions, forming what is essentially an international knowledge bank.

With the help of computer technology and transnational co-operation, journalists have been able to process the Panama data and connect the clues for publication.

The complexity of the issues at hand has required professionals such as lawyers, tax officials, computer engineers and economists to join the team. Investigative journalism has now gained both an international and an interdisciplinary dimension.

This example of solidarity heralds the birth of another opportunity for co-operation: in many countries, journalists are threatened, attacked, imprisoned or killed because of their research. An international network of journalists must be able then to take over the half-finished work of these reporters.

I must take on the work of my colleagues in Mexico who have been murdered for their investigation into relationships between drug smugglers and the police.

And our Mexican colleagues must rush to the aid of the German journalists being investigated for publishing documents implicating the German government in the illegal sale of arms to Mexico.

While German journalists researching the arms trade must complete the investigation into the weapons trafficked into Syria by Turkish intelligence, an exposé that led to my colleague and I being jailed.

This "follow-up" principle must be introduced at a global level. Investigative journalists should not feel alone in the face of threats. The powerful ought to fear that their repressive actions will provoke more international interest and more research.

A media which the powerful believe can be intimidated by censorship, repression and legal damages has more need for investigative journalists and for international solidarity, than ever before.

The disappearance of investigative journalism means uninformed electorates, ordinary people who are unaware of being economically exploited, and dictators prospering because of restrictions on reporting

But teams working together for the public good, who have the bravery to challenge repressive governments and the determination to face down threats, can combine international solidarity and modern information technology.

This is the road of hope which leads from the crossroads at which investigative journalism now stands. ⊗

Translated by John Butler

Can Dündar, *former editor-in-chief of Turkish newspaper Cumhuriyet, was sentenced to five years in prison on a charge of "revealing state secrets" for reporting on sales of weapons by Turkish intelligence to Syrian fighters. He is appealing the verdict. His new book is We Are Arrested (Biteback)*

ABOVE: The 2015 film Truth covered the journalistic investigation into then President George W. Bush's military service

CREDIT: Amr Abdallah Dalsh/Reuters

CULTURE

MAIN: The climate for journalists and writers in Egypt remains restrictive. Here
journalists gesture during their trial at a court in Cairo, in May 2016. Their banner
reads, "Hey press syndicate, why is there no support for 10 of us?"

Bottled-up messages

45(03): 90/95 I DOI: 10.1177/0306422016670356

Author **Basma Abdel Aziz** talks to **Charlotte Bailey** about the dangers of writing fiction in Egypt as the regime becomes increasingly repressive

"**YOU CAN BE** accused of many, many things, and they just keep making it harder for writers. Anyone not agreeing with the regime is considered to be an enemy. It is so hard here." But, as difficult as it is, the prolific Cairo-based writer Basma Abdel Aziz shows no signs of slowing down.

Set in a nameless country, but depicting her native Egypt with eerie accuracy, her

> ### During the last two or three years, it is quite different. Writing my column before the revolution I wasn't facing problems, but now, sometimes, I am facing red lines

dystopic novel, The Queue, was translated from Arabic by Elisabeth Jaquette and had its English-language debut in May – to critical acclaim. But while her work is only now reaching an international audience, Aziz has been a prolific writer of non-fiction and fiction for years. Her collection of short stories, May God Make It Easy, was published in 2007, and the following year saw the publication of her book on police violence in Egypt, The Temptation of Absolute Power. She has been a columnist for Al-Shorouk

newspaper since 2010, criticising the regime in an increasingly difficult environment.

In a new short story, published here in English for the first time, a woman trapped in a glass bottle is able to see, but unable to influence, the world around her. By failing to resist, she views the women, who are concerned only with the superficial details of life, as complicit in the regime. Her inspiration was a pivotal moment of understanding that "we have given away our transient victory to such a totalitarian authority and that we keep turning in the same vicious closed circle, without an end".

The idea, that in an autocratic regime choosing a superficial apolitical life is itself a political act, runs through both this latest story and The Queue. Passive complicity is not something of which Aziz can be accused, but she has found speaking out increasingly difficult.

She said: "During the last three years, or two years, it is quite different. Writing my column before the revolution I wasn't facing problems, but now, sometimes, I am facing red lines telling me 'no, don't do this, don't mention that'."

While the Egyptian constitution, enacted in 2014 following a referendum, enshrines freedom of expression, the penal code has not caught up, and writers and journalists are increasingly being locked up under ill-defined clauses that leave their fate up →

RIGHT: Author
Basma Abdel Aziz

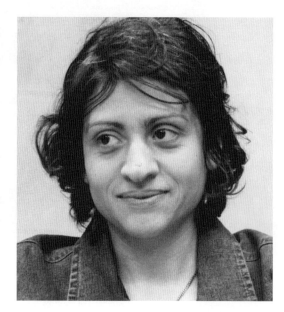

→ to largely conservative judges. According to the Committee to Protect Journalists, 23 journalists were imprisoned in Egypt as of December. Fiction writers also face a deteriorating environment; novelist Ahmed Naji faces two years in prison for "violating public modesty".

Public modesty and blasphemy laws in particular are constraining and punishing writers, but Aziz says all parts of public life work together to enforce the power of Egypt's President Sisi. "Whether you are talking about religion, whether you are talking about politics, whether you are talking about social issues, it is all the same, because all these figures are in unity," she said.

She had believed fiction to be a more permissible way of criticising the regime. But, in May, a friend asked if he could deliver her books to his brother who was in prison. She declined to give him her non-fiction work,

The publishers were also scared and told me they would not publish it. So I kept searching for a publisher that would accept this risk

but said he could take The Queue. The novel, however, was never delivered. Aziz said the responsible officers had told her friend: "This book contains certain ideas and thoughts that are not acceptable."

Nonetheless, for Aziz, fiction remains a powerful way of writing about authoritarianism. "With fiction I am playing on a ground without borders. This fits in well talking about a ruling totalitarian regime, where the citizen's life is transformed [into a] continuous dystopic nightmare, and where [facts] are very hard to find."

Fiction can be a useful medium. In researching her latest non-fiction book, an exploration of military and religious discourse, it was difficult finding people to go on the record. Her research was intended for a master's degree, but the university refused to accept the thesis. So she decided instead to publish the work in a book. "But the publishers were also scared and told me they would not publish it. So I kept searching for a publisher that would accept this risk. I found one, but this is the way things are going now," she said.

Although "a huge number" of her friends are now in prison, she insists the risks will not stop her. "I am continuing to oppose this regime's extreme violence and torture. And I will keep doing it as long as I can."

On the next page, we publish a new short story by Aziz, never previously published in English.

Bottled up

What if I were to start my day on a different footing for a change? I could break my habit of a lifetime and leave the house without my usual cup of tea in the kitchen. What if I tried out being lazy? I could shove aside the reams of paper people are always streaming into the office with. I could just ignore it all and let it pile up and clog up the system – accidentally, of course, on purpose.

Or perhaps I could go and sit in the bathroom, and idle away a couple of hours in there. I could wander aimlessly from one colleague's office to another, stopping here and there for a chat, maybe a cup of coffee or a bite to eat. I'd sit back with a carefree yawn, my notebooks and files piled up in front of me, gnawing on a pencil that splinters between my teeth. I wouldn't bother with any correspondence or with responding to any queries, no matter how pressing. Instead I'd gaze on idly as the people wait, crushed by their exasperation. But why should I feel the need to do anything about it?

I could also let myself go, put on a bit of weight. As my clothes got tighter, my bulging ass would shake when I walk. My stomach would rise in shapely contours, rather than clinging as it does to my spine. No longer would my bones almost protrude from my flesh, grating on

The chatter of girls who have no idea that there is a revolution taking place in the next country, girls who are oblivious to the fact that neighbours have taken to the streets

the metal chair when I sit. Instead, they would be generously cushioned by my ample backside. And I could make the most of my new look to try out new outfits, like flowing skirts and tight, flowery tops with revealing necklines that give a glimpse of my neck and shoulders. And impractical, high-heeled shoes.

I lie in bed a while after waking up and indulge these vivid daydreams. I stretch out my legs and fidget between the warm and cold patches, ignoring the knock at the door and the fact that the cleaning lady might go if I don't let her in. I get up and stretch lazily as I walk to the bathroom. I turn on the tap and wait for the hot water to trickle out, feeling even more relaxed once the knocking stops and I know that I'm on my own. I massage my face with some moisturiser a colleague gave me a few years ago after a trip to the Gulf and which I've never used. Then I sit down and surrender myself to the sun. I ring round my girlfriends to catch up on the TV news and the latest chart hits. The hum of their voices spills into my ear from the handset, the chatter of girls who have no idea that there is a revolution taking place in the next country, girls who are oblivious to that fact that our neighbours have taken to →

→   the streets, that their tyrant has fallen and that others have followed.

Like them I change the channel when the news comes on. I stick plugs in my ears and wander off into the kitchen to make myself a snack. I try not to notice the dust kicked up by all the people falling around me. I get out the vacuum cleaner and run it over everything in my path, trying to suck up the words swirling in the air around me, determined not to let them spoil my new mood.

It isn't long before the vacuum cleaner is full and overflowing. Reaching its bursting point, it starts to spew out everything it has sucked up, choking the space I have just cleared around me. I realise that my attempt to slip out of my skin has come crashing down. The moisturiser hasn't made the slightest difference. A frown beckons, tantalisingly – a scowl that has lurked within me for years. If only I'd just let the chubby cleaning lady in and let her do her job, she would have saved me from having to change everything and I could have carried on with life as it was.

I sit at the table, my elbows resting on the vast quantities of notes I've scribbled. I am always writing one thing or another, because I am overwhelmed by impossible possibilities,

Despite disappearing from the page, these words are still trapped in this bottle. Perhaps someone will find it and crack it open

because their failure to materialise is wearing me down and because their materialisation has become my only dream. And all this time I've been living at the bottom of a huge glass bottle. This bottle is where I wash my clothes, where I eat, where I exercise, where I work, where I write and study and scream out loud. It's where I sleep, where I wake up, where I relieve myself. This bottle is running out of space for me and my non-proverbial excretions; but no matter the pressure, the stopper never pops open to let me pour out. The bottle insists on keeping me trapped inside. When it once decided to expand a little, I relaxed, telling myself I could finally breathe. But it wasn't long before it went back to how it was before – hard and inflexible. It pressed against me so tightly and for so long that I was reduced to a mere figment of myself. Nothing remained of me but a hoarse, broken voice.

I resolved years ago that I'd escape, but I never get anywhere, no matter how I twist and contort myself. I've tried every position, every posture – to no avail. But maybe if I get fat and lazy, if I keep quiet and keep my head down and my skin well moisturised – maybe then the bottle will break.

And while I wait for this bottle to shatter around me, I write about an idyllic day, when

I can finally let my guard down, when I don't need to shout or scream. I walk among the protesters, a little light headed from the exhaust fumes. I buy myself some sugar cane juice and lean against the metal police barrier, the sun beating down, making me frown. But then I half smile, my mouth slightly open. The sugar cane juice has doubled in price, but I pay for it without losing that light-headed, happy feeling. I wipe my lips and throw the paper napkin onto the ground, which is covered in little puddles. I watch the edges of the paper soak up the water. I see the sodden tissue expand and stick to the ground. I wipe my shoes with it until they shine and I walk on in peace.

The sheet of paper I've scrawled on is covered in random, misshapen blobs inching along, trickling from one word to another. Some words have merged, others are illegible. Despite disappearing from the page, these words are still trapped in this bottle. Perhaps someone will find it and crack it open. Perhaps that someone will pour some of the contents down his gullet. And as he belches, the bottle's trapped contents will seep out into the air, filling it with the fresh scent of revolution for everyone to inhale. ⊗

*Translated by **Ruth Ahmedzai Kemp***

***Basma Abdel Aziz** was born in Cairo. She holds a BA in medicine and surgery, an MSc in neuropsychiatry and a diploma in sociology. Her first short story collection, May God Make It Easy, won the 2008 Sawiris Cultural Award. The Temptation of Absolute Power, her sociological study on the effects of police violence in Egypt, was published in 2011 and won the Ahdem Bahaa-Eddin Award for young researchers. She works at the Nadeem Centre for the Rehabilitation of Victims of Torture and as a columnist for Al-Shorouk newspaper*

Muscovite memories

45(03): 96/97 I DOI: 10.1177/0306422016670357

Index publishes the first English translation of a new piece of writing inspired by the reality of Putin's Russia, from one of the country's most lauded poets **Maria Stepanova.** Introduction by **Rachael Jolley**

POET AND JOURNALIST Maria Stepanova is one of the people to watch, but more importantly listen to in today's Russia.

Born in Moscow, Stepanova has won prizes for her poetry, including the Andrey Bely prize, the Joseph Brodsky fellowship, and was awarded a fellowship at Austria's Institut für die Wissenschaften vom Menschen. She admits that time for her poetry has been squeezed by her journalism

work as editor-in-chief of Colta.ru, one of the few independent news websites operating in Russia. Colta, which attracts about 900,000 visitors a month, is a crowdfunded news operation, and is committed to providing an alternative to state-dominated news. Finding time to write creatively is difficult, she said. "I wonder if it is really possible to find a working balance between journalism and poetry. I guess I could also call the combination useful – in terms of 'hurting you into poetry' – but most of the time it simply hurts without any results."

On the eve of the 10th anniversary of the death of Russian investigative journalist Anna Politkovskaya, as journalism in Russia feels particularly vulnerable, Stepanova is more than busy, flat out is a better description, trying to fulfil all these roles.

Index is publishing, below, Stepanova's poem, set against the backdrop of what she describes as "Putin's Russia, penitentiary system, the fragile feeling of brotherhood before the grave". So how does she describe the influences on the writing of this poem? "There is a very distinct background for everything that is happening in contemporary Russia – firstly and mainly, the war in Ukraine.

"But there is more than that. The common sensibility is changing quite rapidly. We are living in a hybrid, multilayered, challenged reality that is mixing visions of the past, fear of the future and endless possibilities of violence and destruction."

And at a historic moment, when we are looking back at Politkovskaya's murder, and all that's happened since in Russia, does she feel any sense of optimism about the next decade? "I am forcing myself to be optimistic with no real reason for it; the situation in the world is even more dark than it used to be 10 years ago. Still, you never know when the eagles are coming." ⊗

The Way It Is

It can be like a tailor but

instead of the straitjacket

(which since childhood so
    longed for fulfilment

cried out to be formed from the canvas)

he sews from a picture

cuts on the bias

a dress, not now constricting
but itching

It can be like a court

in session proceeding

with iron gurney

along a long

clinical corridor

meting out tightly swaddled packages

onerous little life sentences

each three and half
kilogram years
penal umbilical

it can be like bewildered you
    spat out a word

with a hook which lodged

in a comradely body

of wood

in the lip

of a shark

That'll make the line jerk

a fish caught a fish

but the way that it is

a mound 'neath a snowdrift

signifies nothing

inscription on brass

seeing no body

inscription on stone

no matter. We read

he is no more

but here he is

*Translated by **Arch Tait***

Maria Stepanova *is a poet, essayist and journalist. She is the author of 10 poetry collections and two books of essays, and a recipient of several Russian and international literary awards.*

Her poetry has been translated into numerous languages, including English, German, French and Hebrew. She is also the founder and editor-in-chief of an independent online journal, OpenSpace.ru, which she later reconfigured as crowdsourced journal Colta.ru

palgrave
macmillan

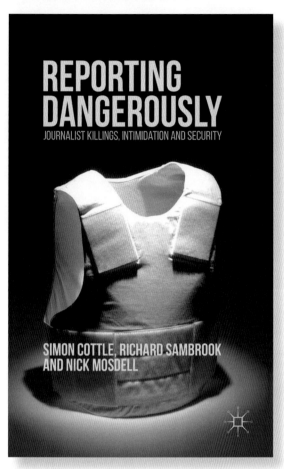

REPORTING DANGEROUSLY
JOURNALIST KILLINGS, INTIMIDATION AND SECURITY

SIMON COTTLE, RICHARD SAMBROOK AND NICK MOSDELL

Hardback | £60 | $95 | 9781137406699
Paperback | £19.99 | $31 | 9781137406729
eBook | £15.99 | $19.99 | 9781137406705

More journalists are being killed, attacked and intimidated than at any time in history. *Reporting Dangerously: Journalist Killings, Intimidation and Security* examines the statistics and looks at the trends in journalist killings and intimidation around the world. It identifies what factors have led to this rise and positions these in historical and global contexts. This important study also provides case studies and first-hand accounts from journalists working in some of the most dangerous places in the world today and seeks to understand the different pressures they must confront. It also examines industry and political responses to these trends and pressures as well as the latest international initiatives aimed at challenging cultures of impunity and keeping journalists safe. Throughout, the authors argue that journalism contributes a vital if often neglected role in the formation and conduct of civil societies. This is why reporting from 'uncivil' places matters and this is why journalists are often positioned in harm's way. The responsibility to report in a globalizing world of crises and human insecurity, and the responsibility to try and keep journalists safe while they do so, it is argued, belongs to us all.

Silence is not golden

45(03): 99/101 | DOI: 10.1177/0306422016670358

Vicky Baker looks back on the controversial career of Chilean-French filmmaker **Alejandro Jodorowsky** and introduces one of his poems on the importance of speaking out

"**W**HAT IS THERE left for someone like me? For a shitty old man like me who thinks cinema is art?" Alejandro Jodorowsky, the French-Chilean filmmaker, poet, author and theatre director, was practically convulsing with fervor as he spat these words into the camera for a crowdfunding campaign to enable him to finish his latest autobiographical film, Poesía Sin Fin (Endless Poetry).

You might not expect an 87-year-old – the winner of multiple awards and a worldwide avant-garde hero for his 1970s cult hits El Topo and The Holy Mountain – to be publically "begging", as he called it. But for Jodorowsky it was preferable to the alternative: complying to the demands of money-hungry commercial studios. In the video he posted online, he promised to keep Poesía Sin Fin true to its roots as an unrestrained art project, "without talking guns, kicks in the head, collapsing buildings, killer robots or super men who have come to show us this is the country that will save the world."

The impassioned plea paid off. The September 2015 campaign was backed by 10,000 donors, raising US$328,102 and covering the previously prohibitive post-production costs.

The film, released this year, is the second part of his autobiographical series. The first was 2013's La Danza de la Realidad (The Dance of Reality), which told of his childhood living with a Stalinist father who fantasised about assassinating Chilean dictator General Carlos Ibáñez del Campo. This latest instalment follows Jodorowsky's teenage years in Santiago. Typical Jodorowsky touches include an actress playing his mother (Pamela Flores) who sings every line as an opera and, in a Freudian twist, later reappears playing his girlfriend, the poet Stella Díaz Varín.

The film focuses on Jodorowsky's first forays into writing poetry. He was 17 when he discovered a typewriter and started to write during the Second World War. Despite being born to Jewish-Ukrainian parents, he felt far from danger, protected by the Andes on one side and the Pacific Ocean on the other. It tells how this era brought friendships with poets such as Gabriela Mistral and Pablo Neruda, who both later won Nobel prizes for literature. "Drunks formed choruses and recited Neruda. Poetry was respected," Jodorowsky told Vice.com. "In Chile, to be a poet was to have a profession: you were a poet. You didn't need to do anything else."

Jodorowsky has had plenty of brushes with the censors in his long career. Full frontal nudity has been either covered up or cut from his films and from his acclaimed comic book series, The Incal. And when his early plays were censored by the government in Mexico, where he also spent a lot of time, he reacted by co-founding Panic Movement, →

ABOVE: Chilean-French filmmaker Alejandro Jodorowsky at the 69th Cannes Film Festival in France on 15 May 2016

→ an uninhibited performance art group in Paris. Having lived in France for much of his life, he has also spoken of losing his friend, the French cartoonist Georges Wolinski, when terrorists stormed the Charlie Hebdo office in Paris. "Wolinsky. *Duele*" ("Wolinsky. It hurts"), he tweeted on the day the artist was murdered in January 2015.

Jodorowsky, once a man with a reclusive reputation who had a two-decade gap from filmmaking, now tweets every day to over a million followers. "Twitter is the literature of our 21st century," he has said. "Better than Haiku. I do it every day now."

The first English translation of his poem What One Must Not Silence is published opposite by Index on Censorship. It was inspired by a quote from Austrian-British philosopher Ludwig Wittgenstein, "Whereof one cannot speak, thereof one must be silent." Jodorowsky argues the opposite: one must speak.

When asked about his inspiration for the poem, Jodorowsky gave Index an equally poetic statement, like a cryptic inner dialogue: "What compelled you to write What One Must Not Silence?
Reason asks questions, the heart gives the answer. What is the essential question?
It doesn't begin, it doesn't end. What is it?
This.
What is 'this'?
Life.
And what is life?
Reason asks questions: words. The heart gives the answer: heartbeats."

What one must not silence

Obliged to live every moment as though on the way back
from a voyage on which treasure was never discovered,
returning to the present, back home with empty hands,
as if it all was still left to do,
as if pausing was no longer being,
and the only way to live was to create utopias,
Wittgenstein, in his Tractatus Logico-Philosophicus, said:
"Whereof one cannot speak, thereof one must be silent."

Yet it is precisely that which cannot be spoken
which must be said aloud,
dipping one's tongue into the invisible changes words
into a mirror,
to set sail in boats we know are without a crew,
taking no further interest in the enigma of what or who
transformed them into phantoms,
an untouchable yet dense presence which we have to
approach like a blind man
within this universe where all is a miracle, or an approximation
made of wax!

In the steps of a blind man plunging his white stick
into the ubiquitous centre,
where the eternal origin of life
bubbles forth.
We can say nothing of this, so all the more reason why in the darkness
he should be our guide.
If we accept our ignorance it becomes a lantern:
beneath its its apparent emptiness, divine flames lie in wait.
Yet here and now nothing remains beyond a look
a few voices, a few fleeting glimmers, and hurrying steps. ⊗

Alejandro Jodorowsky's semi-autobiographical novel, Where the Bird Sings Best, *has been published
by Restless Books*

Poem translated by Amanda Hopkinson

Write man for the job

45(03): 102/107 | DOI: 10.1177/0306422016670359

Index's contributing editor in Turkey, **Kaya Genç**, presents his new short story, written exclusively for this magazine, featuring a failed novelist tasked with reading and flagging the words of supposed dissidents

The Man with the Vermillion Fountain Pen

MR VERMILLION PLACED the bundle of newspapers, magazines and printouts on the wooden table and climbed the bar stool. This was his preferred sitting arrangement, the base from where he directed his operations. A short and slightly hunchbacked man, Mr Vermillion liked to imagine himself having the ideal posture, his back perfectly straight, his chest stretched out to the unknown future, his arms placed on both sides in perfect symmetry, when he sat on that high bar stool. As his Yukari Royale pen (covered in vermillion lacquer, featuring a minimalist trim, it had cost him $1,200) started moving on the sheet placed on top, Mr Vermillion wondered what others in the coffee shop made of him.

He came here every morning. His torpedo-shaped pen, which navigated among letters, words and paragraphs with the graceful moves of a dancer (despite its weight of 45 grams), had earned him the alias Vermillion. It was a useful invention, since he didn't really want to be known in the government circles by his real name and there was something pleasurable in using a pen name for an activity that involved the use of a fountain pen which he had purchased in his youth, when he dreamed of writing fiction with it.

As his hand pressed firmly on the top page (a warm, freshly printed, A4-sized article from a dissident website), Mr Vermillion took joy in imagining himself as someone else. He dreamed of not having the reputation of the unsuccessful writer, which his meager career in Istanbul's literary scene had slowly earned him in the course of the past three decades, but becoming the writer whose power and influence left fellow authors in his shade.

Carefully handling the large white cup, Mr Vermillion took a big sip of freshly brewed coffee and felt lucky to be alive. The smell took him to faraway lands to Egyptian deserts →

→ and African shores and South American jungles where he once imagined, as a young man, placing the characters of his future novels. But distracted he could not allow himself to be at this moment: there were more than 50 columns he had to read before 4pm and his contact in the ministry had told him that his vermillion fountain pen would have the greatest day of its existence, if used properly and according to protocol.

The minister for agriculture had given a roaring speech the previous morning and accused skirt-wearing women of being in cahoots with "ultra-secret ultra-secularists" hidden inside the country. "Our modest women wear skirts only for special celebrations," he had said. "We like our women mature, respectful and silent. And then there are others, the troublemakers..." Mr Vermillion knew in person the speechwriter of the minister and he was in awe of the way that 30-year-old man had designed the speech: the accusation of being a "ultra-secret ultra-secularist" was formulated in such a way that anyone who desired to come to the defence of skirts and women who wore them was automatically labelled *persona non grata*.

The metal section of Mr Vermillion's Yukari Royale pen landed on the paper self confidently, circled a word (the surname of the minister for agriculture) and moved ominously to the next line where its vermillion ink connected that surname to an adjective ("shameless") before reaching the page margin. Once there, the line gave way to a warning (from past experience he knew it would soon become a verdict) in capital letters: SLANDER.

Mr Vermillion's gaze quickly picked words in the adjoining lines that he knew would be even more discriminating in the eyes of the judge who would look at this case. He steered the metal section in the direction of the word "appalling" before the vermillion-coloured line dived lower into the column's penultimate paragraph where it firmly landed around the adjective "foolishly". Mr Vermillion searched passionately for the word "liar" and was disappointed when it turned out that this word (crucial in many court cases) wasn't there. He dreamed of being able to add that insult to the piece.

But there was plenty he could circle with the vermillion ink: a sentence about the minister's private life, another about his elderly, single sister who had a relationship with a Christian pop singer and a third throwaway line about kilt-wearing Scots who, the author said, were respected everywhere for keeping their traditions alive. "I wish the minister, too, would wear a kilt one day," the column's last sentence read.

Why a writer in his mature and, in his eyes, best years would devote himself to producing such rhetoric, Mr Vermillion could never understand. Many of the columnists who now wrote for these dissident publications were novelists and poets during his own youth and rather than growing up to become wise voices, had become child-like. They were able to attract the attention of readers only when they said silly things about silly people, he thought.

Mr Vermillion personally knew the writer whose column he was presently filling with lines and circles and exclamation marks. Once a handsome, witty and self-confident youth with big hopes, this columnist had faced numerous disappointments in middle age (flopped second novel, pulped collection of essays after accusations of plagiarism, harshly criticised script for television drama by the intelligentsia who accused the author of selling out). Now the fate of this man lay in Mr Vermillion's hands.

He placed, on top of the first page, a second article so as not to think about his old friend. This was penned by a former student leader known for his never-ending dislike of politicians and the fierce tone with which he had managed to infuriate anyone from feminists to socialists to sharia supporters during the past 15 years. Mr Vermillion drew a large, red star next to a six-line long paragraph where the author fantasised about the kidnapping of a minister, making a joke about how much the people would enjoy such a development. The whole thing was written in a humorous tone, of course, but the idea to kidnap was there. Next to the star, Mr Vermillion noted how this needed to be interpreted as a concealed threat: fantasising about things were an invitation to doing them. He took another sip from the coffee cup.

Why would middle-aged columnists resort to such rhetoric, he wondered, when they were perfectly free to while away their time writing literary studies or novellas or short stories. Even blurb-writing was a more reputable genre, he believed. In Mr Vermillion's eyes, political columns were the absolute lowest point of literature: he hated those who devoted their lives

Mr Vermillion drew a large, red star next to a six-line long paragraph where the author fantasised about the kidnapping of a minister

to the constant forging of political arguments. Why would anyone be so willing to sacrifice everything in the defence of arguments they had put forward sometime ago because people expected them to put forward one and then defend it day after day, as if they were something other than artificial, self-produced extensions of the artificial art of rhetoric. One's arguments, Mr Vermillion believed, were different from a patch of land, they were not natural, and they did not need physical defending. They were just words and when the timing was right, words could become as dangerous as natural disasters.

As a group of men and women in aqua-coloured suits entered the coffeehouse, Mr Vermillion became conscious of his own presence there. He put the fountain pen to rest, next to the bundle of pages. With its cap on, Yukari Royale was a harmless instrument, an object of beauty and elegance. Mr Vermillion's fingers pushed it a few centimetres away from the pages as if he wanted to take a break from the fountain pen. Now Mr Vermilion looked at the young financiers whose enthusiastic faces pleasantly surprised him. His gaze searched their bodies for signs of youth and found plenty of such signs there – from the tidiness of their garments to the freshness of their appearance they were the image of optimism, energy and hope. How free of bad feeling their bodies were! How unconcernedly they chatted →

→ with one another! How little history they have had behind them and how helpful that last thing was to be in a cheerful mood on a Monday morning.

Mr Vermillion remembered his feeble attempts at producing a political tract as a 17-year-old pupil, when he was at studying at Istanbul's Robert College. Like a minority of rich Turkish kids do in their teenage years, he had adopted socialist ideas so as to distinguish himself from fellow students: it was, Mr Vermillion had felt, the most interesting way of becoming someone different. Among wealthy people, the hatred for wealth set one apart; as a young man Mr Vermillion had excelled at turning that hatred into passionate prose.

In those years Mr Vermillion had loved borrowing words from the socialist glossary. Accusing books and buildings and beautiful paintings of being *petit bourgeois*, emphasising the importance of raising class consciousness, constantly using the words "class conflict" and seeing all phenomena in relation to it – those were the features that defined Mr Vermillion's writing as a young man. After a few tries, he had realised how easy it was to forge a political rhetoric and reproduce it in numberless tracts. Mr Vermillion's skill at writing them as a young man made it easy for his middle-aged self to locate the incriminating content the modern version of such tracts had. In this new era in his life Mr Vermilion would wonder at the

"How stupid," Mr Vermillion mumbled. "How stupid to devote one's time to writing this article, which so clearly spells trouble"

continuity and longevity of the dissident mind. Was it natural that all dissident minds would end up using the same phrases, concepts and the same tone, Mr Vermilion would ask himself, or was it the other way around – was it only because they used the same phrases, concepts and tone that some people were called dissidents?

He placed a weekly news magazine, with a circulation of 4,509 copies, in front of him.

"Made-up charges used to lock up Turkish republicans," the headline of one article read. Mr Vermillion was yawning even before he started reading the opening paragraph of what turned out to be a six-pages long indictment of the charges against "ultra-secret ultra-secularists" hiding in the country.

"How stupid," Mr Vermillion mumbled, and for the first time that morning, raised his head to look outside the coffee shop. "How stupid to devote one's time to writing this article, which so clearly spells trouble."

At a coffee shop on the other side of the street, a young woman with curly blonde hair was listening to something the man sitting next to him was telling her. The woman's eyes followed his every move, and she seemed set to be totally under his influence until the story's completion.

Drawing a large triangle next to the magazine correspondent's name, Mr Vermillion noted: "Potential ultra-secularist." He then wrote a sentence about the correspondent's past activities and was just getting ready to begin another sentence when, much to his chagrin, realised that his Yukari Royale pen had run out of ink.

By the time Mr Vermillion separated his buttocks, numb from sitting too much, from the bar stool, young financiers in the adjoining table were cracking jokes and sharing anecdotes. They all have had their first cups of coffee for the morning and were ready to enjoy the rest of the day.

Mr Vermillion knew from the experience of observing them in the past month that they would leave in about five minutes' time for the office and emerge seven hours later from the sliding doors of the opposite building. Now, as he walked past them, Mr Vermillion distinguished their gazes scrutinising his body – the expression on their faces, Mr Vermillion thought, asked what on earth this elderly man had been doing in this coffee shop every morning for the past few weeks. He imagined them wondering how on earth they had not asked this question before. What did they make of him, he wondered.

Mr Vermillion headed to the loo where he expected some solitude, which he was partly allowed to have. The large mirror on the bathroom wall was perfectly clean; and yet, it framed and reflected his face in a way that the elderly man found disturbing. Mr Vermillion heard the lunch-break bell go off in the high school next door. This was closely followed by the cheering voices of high school kids running around on the long street. Mr Vermillion heard children running in the distance, laughing and cracking jokes and shouting obscenities. Some of them, he knew, would come to the coffee shop to buy lunch. He regretted leaving the Yukari Royale and his bundle of newspapers, magazines and printouts unattended on the table and yet he didn't feel like going back inside. Instead Mr Vermillion looked carefully at the mirror and scrutinised his brow. He looked at the lines formed on that surface, and saw words he had devoted his life to producing and then to criminalising appear as if by magic. Mr Vermillion tried to figure out what the person in the mirror was thinking about. He then opened the little bathroom window and watched a kid walking cheerfully towards the coffee shop. ⊗

Kaya Genç is a contributing editor for Index on Censorship magazine and the author of Under the Shadow: Rage and Revolution in Modern Turkey (I.B.Tauris, September 2016)

Index around the world

INDEX NEWS

45(03): 109/112 I DOI: 10.1177/0306422016670360

From a study of dangers faced by European journalists to a celebration of the power of hip-hop music, **Josie Timms** looks at the highlights of Index's work over the past three months

"**THE BIGGEST THING** I'll take with me is a broader understanding of the ways censorship can affect and hurt people. Searching through the archives has allowed me to see different forms of censorship and how it has evolved. I didn't realise how broad censorship can be," said student Holly Raiborn of her summer working at Index on Censorship's offices. Raiborn and Ianka Bhatia were the first students to take part in a new internship programme created as a partnership between Index and Wellesley College in Massachusetts in the United States. Each year, Index will offer students the opportunity to work across the advocacy, events and editorial teams to gain insight and →

CREDIT: Loranc Sparsi

ABOVE: Colombian hip-hop artist Shhorai performing at the Power of Hip Hop, an event co-produced by Index and In Place of War

RIGHT: The Power of Hip Hop staged performances and talks from a number of hip hop artists, including Poetic Pilgrimage

→ experience into the daily operation of a freedom of expression organisation.

As part of their internships Bhatia and Raiborn completed various tasks, including working on the Mapping Media Freedom project, writing and editing reports, and producing articles for the website. Raiborn collated a special reading list of articles published in Index on Censorship magazine during the South African apartheid years; while Bhatia researched rising censorship in Turkey in the wake of the recently attempted coup.

The two students also both worked closely with the events team to help organise one of the big occasions of the summer: the launch of the 250th issue of Index on Censorship magazine. In July, supporters and friends of Index celebrated 44 years of the magazine with a party at Magculture, a specialist magazine shop in London. Highlights included performances by actor and theatre director Simon Callow, Norwegian musician Moddi and poet Jemima Foxtrot. Louis Blom-Cooper QC, one of Index's earliest supporters, spoke about censorship today.

On their return home to the US, both students will continue their positions on the student advisory board on the Wellesley College Freedom Project, which is dedicated to exploring and debating the idea of freedom.

Index has also continued to work on its UK youth project, What a Liberty! Members presented their Magna Carta 2.0, a modern-day charter covering issues relevant to young people today, at The Collection Museum in Lincoln in July. During the project the group have attended workshops for media training and film-making. The charter was presented to pupils from a Lincoln primary school, sixth-form students and leaders from arts, heritage and education organisations from across the city.

Speaking to school pupils in Lincoln was a highlight for What a Liberty! member Darshan Leslie, who told Index: "It was clear that after showing them the video we produced, they immediately grasped the key messages that we were hoping to share; That it doesn't matter what your age or race or gender is, we are all equal and that this needs

to be reinforced much more rigorously."

It is not only young people the project hopes to spread their message to, they have a much wider audience in mind. Leslie told Index: "We also aim to reach out beyond the younger generation through our use of social media and we hope that within a year we will have expanded our membership and will have the support of prominent figures. So this is very much an evolving project which has much more to deliver."

The Magna Carta 2.0 film will be featured at the Parallax Film Festival in Lincoln during November. They have also been invited to present their project at two schools in London and have been featured in the Lincolnshire Echo. To find out more about future screenings, visit whataliberty.co.uk.

Also in July, Index teamed up with In Place of War, a programme that supports artists living in areas affected by war and conflict, to co-produce The Power of Hip Hop. The two-day event, held at London's Rich Mix arts centre, explored hip hop's influence in today's society.

Sophia Smith-Galer, a member of the Index on Censorship youth advisory board, was among the attendees. "I was a fly on the wall, documenting The Power of Hip Hop as a whole and even getting a chance to interview some of the performers," she said. "I really liked the mix of academia and performance; it gave a genre often regarded as 'guns and girls', as Rodney P [UK hip-hop artist] said in his talk, the intellectual clout that it deserves."

Hearing Colombian rapper Shhorai perform was a particular highlight for Smith-Galer, who said The Power of Hip Hop showed how the genre has a worldwide reach, and often gives a voice to marginalised groups.

She told Index: "What was really unique about The Power of Hip Hop was the showcasing of British artists alongside international ones. For me, that is the sort of initiative we need more of to bust the stereotypes around music that comes from regions we might not be so familiar with in the UK and understanding that all hip-hop artists follow a similar, provocative narrative.

"Bringing them all together in one space showed that hip hop isn't just some disparate

It gave a genre often regarded as "guns and girls" ... the intellectual clout that it deserves

set of unconnected or unknown artists; there is a whole army of them, in a global hip hop community, and they want to be heard."

Smith-Galer produced a podcast of the event for the Index website, featuring a number of artists who performed, including Poetic Pilgrimage (UK) and Zambezi News (Zimbabwe).

Along with Smith-Galer, seven other young people formed the new intake of the Index on Censorship youth advisory →

RIGHT: UK grime
artist Afrikan Boy
also performed at
the Power of Hip
Hop

→ board, serving from July to December. The members of the board, from countries including Hungary, Spain, Germany and the USA, will meet once a month for an online meeting and have the opportunity to write for the website and attend Index events.

Index also took to the stage at Wilderness, a UK festival, in August to explore what you can and can't say in today's society with a taboo-filled game show. Index's events manager David Heinemann and deputy magazine editor Vicky Baker were joined by cartoonist Martin Rowson, comedian Athena Kugblenu, director Nadia Latif and journalist Ian Dunt to debate what were the biggest taboos today.

Using its specially made taboo-o-meter, Index measured the audience's boos to determine which of the topics discussed, including religion, death and the prime minister cavorting with a pig's head, they considered to be taboo. Discussing your own salary did not appear to be so, with nearly all of the audience getting to their feet when asked to shout out their yearly wage.

In July, the third Council of Europe meeting – Journalists at Risk: Part of the Job? – was attended by Index's senior advocacy

Using its specially made taboo-o-meter, Index measured the audience's boos

officer, Melody Patry. Participants discussed a survey that had been circulated to journalists across Council of Europe member states to gather data about unwarranted interference, fear and self-censorship in journalism. The full findings of the survey will be released in a report in April 2017.

Patry said: "Once we have analysed all the data and gained a full picture of the threats, the next step will be to look at the environment in which journalists are working

and see what we can do to improve their situation."

The latest quarterly report of Index's Mapping Media Freedom project, which collects and verifies attacks on journalists, has revealed that across Europe media workers have recently faced an increase in physical assaults. Two murders, 60 incidents of physical assault, 41 incidents of media professionals being detained, 45 criminal charges and civil lawsuits, and 80 verified reports of intimidation were recorded between the months of April and June.

Hannah Machlin, MMF project officer, said: "Violence against journalists has increased overall, but particularly in France during recent protests against new labour laws. Police and demonstrators have been physically harassing journalists, and preventing them from reporting, which is extremely worrying." ⊗

Josie Timms is Index's editorial assistant and chair of the Index on Censorship youth board. She was awarded the first Liverpool John Moores University/Tim Hetherington Fellow at Index

Your Essential Guide to the
Best music from
Around the World

"Music, more than words or literature, has a power to transcend borders and move people. It makes it a very powerful medium, and this is why musicians are so often the target of censorship. *Songlines* magazine is all about politics, history and identity, and the artists who incite change through their music."

Simon Broughton, *Songlines* editor-in-chief

SONGLINES
MAGAZINE

What ever happened to Luther Blissett?

END NOTE

45(03): 114/116 | DOI: 10.1177/0306422016670361

Vicky Baker looks at the enduring legacy of a 1990s collective of Italian writers and activists, who carried out a series of media hoaxes in the name of a Watford FC footballer

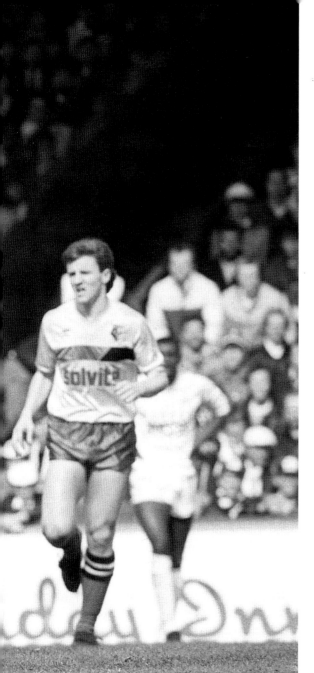

fuck the Luther Blissett Project!" shouted a protester when a brawl broke out in an Italian bookshop at the tail end of last year. The conflict had started with some eye rolling, mumbled swearing and ssshhing during a reading. Then tempers rose. Before long, the speaker had risen to his feet, moved towards a particularly disruptive audience member in a black hoodie, and launched some punches. The reason? The speaker had declared that "artivist" Luther Blissett was back, and some people clearly didn't agree.

The original Luther Blissett collective committed ritual suicide almost 17 years ago. The group of Italian cultural activists decided enough was enough. Together they had written books, including best-selling historical thriller Q, and conducted a stream of media pranks, such as convincing an Italian TV programme to cover the disappearance of British conceptual artist, Harry Kipper, who had gone missing while biking along the Italian-Yugoslav border. (Harry Kipper didn't exist. And neither did Loota, the fe-

LEFT: Luther Blissett playing for Watford FC against Tottenham Hotspur in 1987

The project lasted five years ... but their curious slogan, "Be Luther Blissett", ran out of their hands

"LUTHER BLISSETT IS nobody... and everybody!" said Constantinos Tachtsidis, a journalist and musician from Greece who runs the Luther Blissett Music Project. Since 2009, he has been collaborating with musicians across the country, producing and sharing songs under the same name: Luther Blissett. His project was inspired by a 1990s Italian activist group, which was, in turn, oddly inspired by an English footballer whose name was appropriated as the collective's pseudonym. "It is something like a guerilla war on the cultural industry," Tachtsidis told Index.

"Long live the Luther Blissett dissidents,

male chimpanzee they said would exhibiting at the 1995 Venice Biennale of Contemporary Arts.)

The fight in the Rome bookshop happened last November during the launch of a new title, The Luther Blissett Project in Rome: 1995 to 1999. The book uncovers lesser-known stories of offshoot activities in the capital, away from the founders' base in Bologna. On YouTube, footage of the bookshop fight includes a footnote mentioning Rome theatre group, Dynamis Teatro, implying that this too might have been a stunt.

"You guessed right," Dynamis Teatro's Valentina Vaccarini told Index. "The →

→ audience didn't know it was staged. In fact, most of them were embarrassed and some were nervous about what was going on."

"I am Luther Blissett. I have organised and performed the event at the bookshop," wrote an Italian activist, who wished to remain anonymous, in an email to Index. They insisted a clear distinction should now been drawn between the obsolete Luther Blissett Project and the collective pseudonym Luther Blissett, which is still in use today. "In Italy you can find an indefinite number of individuals making use of this name for political, cultural and artistic activities."

Roberto Bui, one of the founders of the original project, told Index they are fed up with being asked about Luther Blissett. "For us, it's archaeology," he said. They ensured

In Italy you can find an indefinite number of individuals making use of the name Luther Blissett for political, cultural and artistic activities

the project only lasted five years, as a nod to Stalin's first five-year plan to collectivise the Soviet economy, but their curious slogan, "Be Luther Blissett", soon ran out of their hands and others, including Tachtsidis in Greece, have been picking up on it ever since. This was always the intention. Bui and his colleagues produced all their works under a "copyleft" policy – ie the antithesis of copyright and a precursor to Creative Commons licensing.

Marco Deseriis, author of the book Improper Names: Collective Pseudonyms from the Luddites to Anonymous, believes the motivations behind using a collective pseudonym go beyond simply wanting to mask

an identity. "Only a handful of shared pseudonyms have gained international notoriety," he told Index. "This is due to the fact that these pseudonyms emerge in times of crisis, when other forms of representation are precluded. Yet we can say that pseudonyms such as Luther Blissett and Anonymous have influenced, perhaps indirectly, a variety of actors." He cites movements and grassroots organisations including the Tea Party, Occupy, and Black Lives Matter, which may experience disagreements over use of their name, "a practice that is accelerated and made highly visible by the hashtag politics of social media".

As for the original founders of the Luther Blissett Project, they went on to found the Wu Ming Foundation in 2000 and have continued to write collectively, albeit now with only three of the original five members. Their identities are not a guarded secret, although Wu Ming – which means anonymous in Mandarin – is a common byline for dissidents in China. It was a pseudonym for director Wang Xiaoshuai for his 1997 film Frozen, which was banned in China after he screened his previous film internationally without government approval.

Meanwhile, in the UK, the real Luther Blissett is very much alive and well. The former Watford Football Club and AC Milan striker had his name appropriated for reasons he's never quite understood, but he has come to accept it. As he said to Italian journalist Malcom Pagani: "The first time I heard about this thing, I didn't want to believe it. To think that someone, a group or a single person, could take on my name seemed ridiculous. I've never wanted to be anyone other than myself in my life. Then I reflected on it and I was happy. It was like leaving a sign of my passage, a fingerprint, a stone left behind on a street." ⊗

Vicky Baker is deputy editor of Index on Censorship magazine. She tweets @vickybaker